Shattered Dreams

Bill O'Brien was born in Wellington in 1946 and joined the police in 1963. During a career spanning three decades he has regularly seen the effects of serious crime on the victim. Since moving to Dunedin in 1989 he has been on the executive of the Victim Support Group and held the post of chairman during the writing of this book. He is now even more acutely aware of the need for victim support, particularly in cases of homicide.

Shattered Dreams

Families of New Zealand Murder Victims Speak Out

Bill O'Brien

DL

David Ling Publishing Limited
PO Box 34-601
Birkenhead, Auckland 10

Distributed in New Zealand by Forrester Books
Glenfield, Auckland 10

Shattered Dreams

ISBN 0-908990-36-7

First Published 1996
Reprinted 1996

© Bill O'Brien 1996

Typeset by ExPress communications Limited
Printed in New Zealand

Dedications

To Lynley, Debbie and Donna whose foresight and determination led to the formation of the support group Family and Friends of Murder Victims and to the memory of those loved ones murdered in New Zealand.

Acknowledgements

I wish to sincerely thank the families of those victims whose stories appear in this book. The re-telling of the effects of horrific crimes on them and their families took courage and their co-operation in telling what is essentially 'their' story is very much appreciated.

Major thanks however must go to Lynley Illingworth, Donna Perrin and Debbie Francis from Owaka who, at the suggestion of some families, had the vision for their stories to be recorded. Much of the background research is as a result of their efforts.

To Dame Ann Ballin, Chairperson of The Victims' Task Force, for providing a foreword and John Miller of Victoria University's Law Faculty for his expert guidance on accident rehabilitation and compensation.

As in previous works thanks must go to my wife Olwyn and daughter Lauren for their typing and editing skills.

Contents

Foreword

The inevitability of death – our own and that of people we love and care about – is an issue we must all deal with. The grief, the bewilderment, the sense of loss, the anger, are all part of human experience. Try as we might, with all that technology has achieved, we must encounter it in the end and hope that we can deal with it. Most of us do in our various ways as we ponder on illness, pain and death with those around us having some understanding of the process we are trying to manage.

However, there are times when facing the death of a family member or close friend takes on a different dimension. The violent destruction of a life by one or more people has a much greater traumatic effect than death by disease. Common responses are exacerbated by rage, confusion, loss of control, loss of trust in community morality and many other responses which are reflected in this book. These are the normal reactions to abnormal acts and should be supported as such by the law and public institutions.

Families and friends of victims of murder and manslaughter have many needs which should be met if they are to regain some peace of mind. They have the right to this rather than spending large parts of their lives struggling with anxiety and doubt about the meaning of such tragic events.

The Victims of Offences Act 1987 allows for these supports but co-ordination of services and regulations lag behind the practical provision of what measures we believe necessary. The lack of the strong presence of a Commissioner for Victims makes the sustained provision of pertinent information to Government and police very difficult, if not impossible. If such a position existed, it would also be possible to monitor various aspects of the Criminal Justice system to observe the positive and negative issues which affect the lives of the bereaved.

The generous co-operation of the families represented in this book should provide the New Zealand public with some insight into the human realities of death by murder or manslaughter. And although it is never possible to understand fully what such an experience is like, I hope that what understanding readers do gain will stimulate them to demand more appropriate support for this group of victims.

Dame Ann Ballin

Preface

When I was approached to write this book I must admit to initial doubts about the wisdom of writing what is essentially a very sad book. However I was quickly convinced by the families of those who had died that there was a need for such a book. Throughout their stories similar themes emerge that are so common, yet so disturbing it is essential we all understand. None of them would wish or have ever contemplated being thrust into the turmoil of a family homicide. This is a collection of their stories, how their lives have been affected forever and shows how none of us are immune from becoming unwillingly involved. Those whose stories appear in this book would, like the reader, believe it only happens to others.

I am also pleased to have been involved in writing this book to help support the organisation Family and Friends of Murder Victims. Their work has finally begun to see changes in law, attitudes and assistance to those left to grieve after the tragedy of a homicide in their family.

Hopefully the production of this book will continue the movement to recognise the special needs of families left shattered by these horrific crimes.

Prologue

On 1 November 1991 the tiny South Otago town of Owaka was torn apart. Kylie Smith, a talented, attractive 15-year-old went riding on her horse. For this highly capable horsewoman it was a usual practice but on this occasion Kylie never returned. Instead she was callously raped and murdered by a man at the time on bail awaiting a court appearance for a serious sexual offence.

Without ever contemplating such an event the family and friends of Kylie were plunged headlong into a nightmare that can never really end.

Three local Owaka women were so distressed at the loss of Kylie Smith they decided on a course of action to ensure homicide victims' families and their friends could be better supported and the perpetrators of these shocking crimes should be made fully accountable.

They were neither vindictive nor emotional. They simply wanted justice to be done. Throughout the difficulties with officialdom and despite being labelled reactionary in some quarters, the ladies steadfastly continued with their quest. Through their persistence and genuineness they are beginning to make a difference.

Arising out of this terrible crime grew the organisation Family and Friends of Murder Victims. They began by organising one of this country's biggest petitions to address inequities in the law. Their persistence has seen changes to the sentencing ranges judges can now impose on murderers by ensuring minimum periods of imprisonment are enforced. Changes to ACC legislation and some victim support issues can in part be attributable to them.

Hopefully the death of Kylie will not be totally in vain. While the cherished daughter of Bevan and Dawn Smith can never be returned, her loss might well be the catalyst for at last getting to grips with a shadow that darkens what many regard as "Godzone".

Perhaps too, readers of this book will realise that so often the victims of murder are totally innocent. Some have been the targets of callous killers and just happened to be in the wrong place at the wrong time. None of them deserved to die, yet in many cases an unfeeling public is quick to pre-judge. What did the victim do to get into such a position? If they hadn't gone there this wouldn't have happened! It's probably their fault anyway! Such beliefs are so far from reality and do nothing to support families suddenly torn apart.

Not only do the circumstances sometimes get displaced in the minds of others but so does the apportioning of blame. Throughout this book there is a common thread. Too often the excuse for an offender's actions gets put on to the victim, almost as if to absolve the offender of blame. Too often families have been hounded by phone, letter or in person by the offender, or ones close to them, again trying to shift blame or make the victim's family shoulder some of the responsibility. Academics can debate the reasons why some see such a need to displace the blame. Readers of this book should be left in no doubt that there are victims of homicides and perpetrators of these crimes. We should not be confused as to who is who.

1

The Petition

When the *Sunday Times* of 31 January, 1993 was published it carried a graphic, full page advertisement exhorting people to watch that night's TV3 programme *20/20*.

Dark, stormy clouds surround a tuft of grass with a small wooden cross emblazoned with the name Kylie Ann Smith. In large lettering on the dark background were two simple sentences. IF KYLIE CRIED FOR HELP AS SHE WAS BEING RAPED, NOBODY HEARD. IS ANYONE LISTENING NOW?

At the time many people were listening, but like everything else, people tend to forget as they get on with their lives. But back in the South Otago township of Owaka a band of dedicated people fight to ensure we do listen, that we don't forget. Soon after the pride of this small community was raped and murdered a groundswell of public outrage began and swept throughout New Zealand. This was an outrage at the criminal justice system, at a lack of compensation for the family members of those murdered and more importantly a desire to see that the perpetrators of such horrific crimes did in fact pay their debt. Although it was the death of 15-year-old Kylie Smith that became the catalyst for a massive petition, hers wasn't the only death that has outraged New Zealanders. We have been sickened by murders such as the killing of 6-year-old Theresa Cormack in Napier; Kirsa

Kylie Ann Smith with Timmy in 1990.

Bevan Smith and Debbie Francis carry the banner of the parade led by Donna Perrin, Dawn Smith and Lynley Illingworth.

Jensen, also of Napier, taken from her horse in broad daylight with her body still remaining unrecovered. The schoolgirl Karla Cardno, abducted and murdered after visiting a dairy in the Lower Hutt suburb of Taita; Louisa Damadran, a little girl killed and thrown into a river in Christchurch. Another small child, Sarah Currie of Invercargill, who was sexually molested and murdered. Or the 83-year-old widow Nora Sole, raped and murdered in the inner sanctuary of her own home. These are but a handful of the dreadful crimes that spring to mind in New Zealand, a country we are so proud of.

Disgraceful as all of these crimes are, it seems that the outrage on Kylie Smith was what tipped the balance. And from the people of Owaka came the seeds of dissent that have gained phenomenal support. As the horrific account of Kylie's murder unfolded, people like Bevan and Dawn Smith were grateful of a vehicle to help vent their bitterness and frustration at the criminal justice system as they saw it. Enter Debbie Francis, a resident of Owaka for only two years. She was so affected by the Kylie Smith murder she approached Bevan and Dawn with an offer of support. Not the clamour for revenge against the murderer that some have associated with the call for longer sentences, but rather out of compassion and concern. Debbie was not only a short-term resident of Owaka but relatively new to New

Zealand. Born in South Africa, she had pursued a career as a nurse prior to meeting her Kiwi husband. They returned to New Zealand in 1978 and farmed in the family partnership in Central Otago before buying their own farm in Owaka.

When the full realisation of Kylie's murder hit home people became numb. Numbed by the shocking realisation that something so violent and horrible could happen in their safe little haven. Looking into the faces of their friends and seeing the raw pain in their eyes drove Debbie Francis and two other women to do something that was to ultimately change their lives. Joining Debbie were two longer residing Owaka women. Lynley Illingworth was born in Bluff but had grown up in the Catlins since the age of six. After leaving Owaka District High School she trained as a kindergarten teacher, taking up a teaching post in Wellington for 13 years. Returning to Owaka she married a farmer and lives there with Trevor and her two daughters. She has for the past five years been supervisor at the Owaka Playcentre. Donna Perrin, a Dunedin born and raised woman, moved to South Otago 14 years ago working for a time in the ANZ Bank and later in the small Owaka hospital. Her husband, Alistair, is a local transport owner and operator and cousin of Bevan Smith. Alistair Perrin was groomsman at Bevan and Dawn's wedding and his wife is now one of the driving forces in seeing justice is served to the family and friends of murder victims.

While the three had a burning desire to help the Smiths come to grips with their tragedy, they could never have contemplated that their honest intentions would lead to huge drains on their time, finances and families. Little did they realise that the process of preparing a petition to parliament would become a catalyst for literally hundreds of victims. The family and friends of many murder victims, killed over recent years, had been left feeling that the "system" had looked after the murderer with the victims seemingly uncared for. Out of the petition sprang a support group called Family and Friends of Murder Victims. Although Owaka-based they have other branches in New Zealand with many members giving them a chance of support and to gain solace from each other. After all these are people with very special needs. Losing a loved one is always stressful. To do so under unusual circumstances or in major catastrophes adds a further dimension. But losing a close relative or friend to murder, more especially in the nature of Kylie Smith's case, the dimension increases incredibly. Almost immediately the three Owaka women began circulating their petition, a huge groundswell of support began and the families of murder victims all around New Zealand suddenly came forward to say yes, we need help, we need support. At last they had a voice, an identity and any thoughts that Debbie, Donna and Lynley had of seeing their work finished when a petition was presented suddenly flew out the window.

Taking on something as ambitious as a petition calling for life sentences to mean life, hurtled the three into the full glare of publicity. And three rather ordinary, well-intentioned country women were suddenly the centre of attention, and it wasn't all good publicity. When one starts "rocking the boat" for change not everyone agrees. Before long the criminologists, academics and those with a civil liberties leaning, not to mention some politicians, viewed the work with suspicion. Before long allegations of rednecking, vengefulness and mob rule were to be levelled at the women. But those who levelled the accusations certainly weren't listening to the people as one of this country's biggest petitions gained momentum.

All of the associated publicity and having to defend themselves against more eloquent and academic opponents was not easy. Never before had any of the three fronted television. They were unused to talking to the media and certainly not used to having to defend themselves for doing something they honestly believed in. Yet despite the ups and downs, the pointed fingers and the labelling their resolve had never faulted. At no stage did any of the three women ever envisage the amount of publicity they would receive. And furthermore they never wanted it. However, they now realise that if you hope to achieve anything on this scale you have to take the good with the bad and to their credit that's what they have done. Debbie Francis can remember in the early days, if she could just sit in a dark cupboard and pass bits of paper out to achieve their objectives she would be quite happy. It wasn't the media attention alone that made them nervous. They were dealing with such a serious topic affecting so many lives that Debbie Francis can still remember how her heart would start pumping and mouth dry up as soon as the interviewer's cameras went on. They weren't talking about a problem of potholes in the road, this was serious and they had to be so careful that what they said came out right.

To present a petition to parliament takes an effort. If it is a small petition it takes a big effort. If it's a big petition it takes a monumental effort. When parliament sat on 22 February, 1993 a number of petitions were presented. They ranged from a Kirsten McKenzie and 60 others asking government to promote arts and culture, through to opposition against introducing European rabbit fleas, while another opposed alcohol advertising. A fairly large petition of a Jacqueline and Anthony Pearson and 4,150 others asked government to limit sexual material on view to children.

But on that day another petition was presented. It asked for life imprisonment for those given life sentences and no bail for serious sexual offenders. The petition, presented by Debra Ann Francis, Donna Leanne Perrin and Lynley Dawn Illingworth was supported by 271,223 other people. By any standards this petition was massive and even more spectacular when one thinks that it was achieved in three dining rooms in a tiny South Island town of only 400 people.

This huge public clamour for a sentence reflecting the seriousness of premeditated murder was not the product of some organisation with unlimited resources and finance. How then, could three inexperienced people with such limited resources gain such a public response? Not easily and only hard work, sacrifices and a desire to succeed kept them going. The overwhelming support that gained momentum as word of the petition spread across New Zealand helped their cause no end. While Bevan and Dawn Smith gained solace from the support being offered, Bevan was particularly concerned about the ethics. What stabbed him was that the whole petition was generated there in Owaka, in those three dining rooms. He was mindful of the amount of money the huge mailouts would have cost the three women. Realising the financial strain this must have placed on the three local women he found it hard to rationalise that the justice department had an advertisement in the Tender columns of the *Otago Daily Times* offering financial assistance to anyone associated with the rehabilitation of offenders. That was the sort of irony that Bevan Smith believes emphasises that resources are going into helping offenders rather than the victims and an anomaly he wants to see changed.

Funding came from many sources but almost all of them were victims who wanted to express their frustrations and feelings. A $10 note here or a $100 there would certainly help, but the amount spent by the three petitioners themselves will only be known by them, and they are not saying.

To get a petition going, the women had to write a monumental number of letters. The very first move was from Debbie Francis, writing to the editors of every metropolitan and provincial newspaper in New Zealand. She believed that they would not accept copied letters so decided to handwrite all 50 of them. As she was writing she spoke to Lynley Illingworth and said she was sitting down and writing so many letters. Offering to help, Lynley took over some of the letter writing and at that time Donna Perrin came on to the scene to also share in the task and it was from that moment that the team was formed, a team that's gone from strength to strength. All but one newspaper printed the letters and it was that one, the *Otago Daily Times*, which made the women cross. Donna Perrin recalled that when they did finally publish they left the obvious part of the letter out, that was calling for people to sign a petition. It was then that the three realised that to get the support they needed they had little alternative but to write to as many people as they possibly could.

Getting the petition pages out to the public was a more challenging job. Sitting in their Owaka homes the women wrote volumes. For example, they got the Auckland telephone book and thumbed through the Yellow Pages writing to every takeaway bar, dairy, liquor outlet, pet shop, video parlour and other similar establishments asking that they put the petition on their counter. They asked that the pages be sent back when completed and enclosed a stamped, self-addressed envelope with each letter. That process went on throughout many other centres around New Zealand and took months of painstaking work at night.

Next came the marathon effort of writing to people for support, something the three women found difficult. They had never ever done that sort of thing before, they didn't like to ask for money and certainly they didn't want to accept it even when it was offered. But the letters, faxes and telephone calls around the country would have meant that they could not succeed without some assistance and they were grateful for the support they got. They wrote to all sorts of companies and organisations they thought could help. Support for the signing of the petition was sought from the fire service, nurses, police stations and the army. The women hoped to get help from large sectors of the community and were hoping that organisations like the Police Association could push the idea to their members. Apart from the army who denied access to the petitioners other large organisations were only too happy to help.

Despite the tremendous amount of work there was no flagging of interest or spirit and with the 1/4 million-plus signatures the three petitioners, accompanied by Bevan and Dawn Smith, headed for

Wellington and a march on parliament. The five were not alone. Out of the township of only 400 people, over 50 locals got on the plane to lend support in the march from Wellington Civic Centre to the Beehive. The local publican, the shearing contractor, the Owaka policeman, school community staff, friends and others all converged on the capital, all paying their own way. Support in Wellington was swelled by a large number of concerned citizens and even bigger numbers of people, just like the Smiths. Pam Wadsworth whose daughter Jayne had been raped and murdered in Dunedin, the parents and wife of Danny Fleming killed at Hokio on New Year's Day 1992. David and Beth Merryweather who lost their son, Craig, to murderers in the South Island and many others. Each one had a story of heartbreak to tell. Of loved ones gone forever, often in most brutal ways. And some of those whose grieving is still going on stood in support of the petition while the killers, sentenced to life imprisonment, were already released back into the community.

Obviously not everyone in Owaka could afford to travel to Wellington and march in support of the petition. Although over 10% of the tiny town's population made the long trek, those remaining behind needed to show their support in a tangible way. With numbers swelled from around South Otago, over 500 people marched from the Catlins Area School to the town centre clearly showing their support for the Smiths and the petition. Pipers from the Balclutha Highland Band led the parade, their music pausing as they moved silently past Kylie's home and again at the fire station where concerned residents had gathered the previous November to search for the missing schoolgirl. The march ended with a simple prayer for the petition's success offered by one of Kylie's former classmates.

One could assume that having gathered so many signatures and successfully presenting it that that would be the end of the effort, but it was far from over. Such was the support and the identifying of so many frustrated victims of murder that a national organisation, Family and Friends of Murder Victims was set up with branches throughout New Zealand. At last people would have the courage to speak out about how they felt. At last they had the support of others to help with the anger, frustration and torment associated with death by murder. Whenever someone takes on an issue, particularly such an emotive issue as sentencing violent criminals, it not only gains support but also the detractors. It was almost as if some believed the petitioners had ulterior motives. It seemed easy to knock the efforts by labelling the women as rednecks, vengeful and over-emotional. This angered them as their only desire was to present to parliament what the New Zealand people were saying. After all, 271,000 plus people signed the petition and by any stretch of the imagination that was a lot. Bevan Smith believes that had the women had the resources of a large organisation and had they been able to get to every town in New Zealand a million signatures could have been gained.

Instead support from those who should have helped could not always be relied on. The biggest disappointment the petitioners had was the Minister of Justice, Doug Graham. Frequently he made statements which not only disappointed the three women but angered them.

Dawn Smith and the Minister of Justice the Hon. Doug Graham with some of the near 300,000 petition signatures.

Immediately after the petition had been presented Dawn Smith was asked to pose with Doug Graham beside the stack of petition forms. This was immediately after a number of victims had told of their stories of heartbreak.

"Doug Graham had the audacity to ask me if the Police Association had funded us," Dawn said. "I was so mad I could have kicked him."

She is still smarting over what she thought was a most inappropriate comment. Mr Graham should have known that the petitioners had done all the work themselves with some donations coming in from individuals. The Police Association had in fact donated an advertisement for which the women were grateful, and that was probably what Doug Graham latched on to, thinking they were paying for everything. Lynley, Donna and Debbie were far from impressed, especially at his timing.

Early in the collection of signatures, Mr Graham made a statement which again caused the women's ire to be raised. So angry had he made

21

them that they replied to his criticism and had a copy of their letter published in a newspaper. Their reply was quite clear.

As organisers of the petition for harsher penalties we would like to make public our reply to statements made by the Minister of Justice in the *Sunday News*. Dear Mr Graham, we are absolutely outraged at your statements in the *Sunday News* of September 20, 1992 on page 9 in the article "Why life is not enough."

Firstly when you saw Mr and Mrs Smith they told you about our petition and you said, "By all means go for it." Now three months later you state it is just a non-starter. It appears that even if we got every New Zealander to sign the petition you would flippantly disregard what we want. It would also appear that we have been totally ignorant in our belief that politicians are there to listen to the people and to change grossly inadequate laws if this is what we want.

Secondly it is abhorrent the way you describe domestic violence in the article. We are utterly disgusted that you can say "Some chap that clocks his wife in a fit of depression, financial hardship and down she goes, hits her head and dies." From the Minister of Justice a statement like that can only leave the country wondering where we are heading. It also seems that you have not read the petition. We did not ask that every murderer be put away for life. Only brutal murderers who we describe as cold, calculated, deliberate murderers of innocent people. We also asked that no bail be given to first time serious sexual offenders regardless of them having a prior conviction. It is unbelievable that some defence counsel can describe thousands of decent citizens demanding changes to the ludicrous laws as "the clamour of the mob." We feel strongly that these lawyers are influenced by the people in high places such as yourself. Your flippant statements do not set a good example.

We intend forwarding copies of this letter to radio and newspapers. We can honestly say that as law abiding, decent citizens we feel very disillusioned with the state of the justice system in this country. How many more families have to suffer the hellish pain when their loved ones are murdered simply in the name of justice for the criminals?

It would not surprise us if people took the law into their own hands as the laws presently let us all down so badly. Quite simply we and thousands of others have literally had enough. Sincerely, Debra Francis, Donna Perrin and Lynley Illingworth.

In a way the comments of Doug Graham became perplexing. On one hand he seemed doubtful of the women's motives or intentions, yet he was clearly reported as supporting heavier penalties. In one news report Attorney General Paul East called for jail terms up to 25 years for murder. Mr East had claimed that for certain types of murder it wasn't right that someone could be eligible for parole after only 10 years.

"By the time parole is considered the circumstances of the offence have often faded into history," he had said. "It would be far better, in my view, to set the term of imprisonment to be served at the time of sentencing when all the circumstances are placed before the court."

Mr East was referring to murder cases involving sexual molestation and killing of children, police officers on duty and contract killings by underworld figures. In the same report Mr Graham was quoted to have said, without specifying sentencing lengths, "I am a little surprised frankly that we have continued over the last 50 years or so with one sentence for murder no matter how it was committed."

That was exactly what Donna, Debbie and Lynley were hoping to achieve and Mr Graham's inconsistencies left them quite bewildered. The pain and frustrations of those victims left behind was the driving motivation. Despite the labelling from some quarters none of the motives were vengeful. Of course the women are emotional, who couldn't be when knowing the full horror of Kylie Smith's death. But they are decent, concerned citizens who, like hundreds of thousands of us, have had enough of the inequities in our increasingly violent society. They have the concerns of the hundreds belonging to the Family and Friends of Murder Victims support group at heart, and it is for them the three women feel the need to carry on. It was for those people that caused Donna Perrin to attack further comments made by Mr Graham. In a letter replying to a question of counselling for murder case victims, Mr Graham likened such crimes to accidents. In his letter to Donna Perrin of 13 October 1993, Mr Graham said,

Dear Donna Perrin, I am writing in response of your letter of 5 September regarding compensation for the families of victims. I agree that to be a victim of crime can be a frightful experience.

The trauma involved in being a friend or family member of a homicide victim may be intense and require counselling. It is similar, however, to the trauma of a parent whose child has been killed through another cause such as an automobile accident. Both go through a similar grieving process and will require similar support to carry on with their lives. Of course, much support will derive from family and friends.

However it seems inequitable to give one grieving parent preferential access to support over another based solely on the cause of death of their child.

It is for this reason that I believe that potential compensation for parents or friends of victims of crime should remain within the ambit of the Accident Rehabilitation and Compensation Insurance Corporation.

Donna was infuriated. While she and the others know clearly how traumatic the loss of anyone is, murder cases are *different*. Never have they sought to minimise the loss of a child in an accident, but they know that the pressures faced, particularly in a well-publicised homicide, are different. Consequently different circumstances dictate different assistance.

So from small, well-intentioned beginnings grew one of New Zealand's biggest petitions, a new support for the family and friends of those who died from murder and a constant bureaucratic battle to fight for justice.

Donna, Debbie and Lynley are still very much united. They have achieved a great deal but realise there is still a long way to go. Even if someone were to take over the reigns of the support group the trio would not rest until sentences for murderers are equated to their crime. Some will call it vengeance, others might call it the clamour of the mob. For three honest, caring and very dedicated Owaka women it is simply justice.

2

Kylie Smith

After school on 1 November, 1991, 15-year-old Kylie Smith rode her horse out of the tiny South Otago settlement of Owaka. She never returned. Kylie had been abducted by a man on bail for a serious sex offence. He drove Kylie miles from home, forced her at gunpoint up a bank where he raped, murdered and tried to conceal her body. The murderer was arrested and is serving life in prison.

When Owaka plumber Bevan Smith accepted a job at the local chemist shop he thought little of it. Although it meant a lawn had to be excavated to lay pipes it wasn't unusual and anyway on hand was a young man employed to help clean up the section on completion of the work. Although the two men worked together for three or four hours, very few words passed between them. The younger man was quiet and kept to himself. As they worked the chemist's wife made afternoon tea and invited the younger man in for a break. Yet no invitation was extended to Bevan Smith, not because he was unapproachable, on the contrary. Bevan Smith was not a Baptist. And that is what sticks in Bevan Smith's mind. For this man, working with him, was living in Owaka under the watchful eye of the local Baptist community. Within 24 hours he was to abduct, rape and then callously murder Bevan's cherished daughter Kylie.

When Kylie Smith died New Zealanders were outraged and rightly so. For Kylie wasn't an ordinary young lady and this dreadful crime was no ordinary crime. It was a cold, calculated and well planned offence so foreign to decent thinking humans that it's hard to comprehend. When Dawn Smith talks of Kylie she does so with a deep sadness but with a mother's obvious pride. Dawn teaches at the Catlins Area School, a school where Owaka children and those from the outlying farming community go. Little 5-year-olds mixing with what must seem to them huge 18-year-olds, yet enjoying the family atmosphere only an area school can provide.

When the school magazine of 1991 was printed the back page was devoted to one of their most popular students. Next to it was the yearly prize list and it makes dreadfully sad reading. And what made Kylie so special? This 15-year-old was just about to finish her fourth form year and had her name at the top of her year's prize list. Excellence in English, Mathematics, French, Social Studies and Physical Education. That was nothing unusual as the talented youngster's name appeared in similar prize lists for the three previous years. The Catlins Area School boasts a fine choir and musical group. Kylie featured in both, not to mention roles in theatrical productions of the school. A Duke of Edinburgh Bronze Award candidate, member of the *Catlins Post* production team, school council representative, class captain and winner of a Rotary speech contest were Kylie's academic achievements. In the year she died she also took out second place in the *Jean Family Trust* Disability Essay Competition.

Kylie's impressive academic record was, however, no match for her sporting endeavours. From the time this impressive young woman was in Standard IV she was a South Otago representative and captain at netball, a position she kept right up until her death. She was an Under 15 swimming champion and very capable at cross country. But Kylie Smith's first love was the Pony Club and her bedroom, untouched since her tragic death, remains as she decorated it. On every wall are ribbons and photographs won in competition and put up with pride by a youngster regarded as one of Otago and Southland's best riders. Everything was there from dressage, showjumping and eventing, not to mention Best Rider awards. Of all the aims and ambitions Kylie had her burning desire was to ride for New Zealand at the Olympic Games.

Kylie will never achieve those ambitions, her life being taken by someone who should never have even been in a position to harm her.

26

Kylie on Nick prior to a dressage tournament in Mosgiel the year she died.

Paul David Bailey was working alongside Kylie's father solely because of the influence of members of the local Baptist Church. And what angers and haunts Bevan Smith is that Bailey had no right to be in Owaka. He was on bail for attempting to rape a woman in the Central Otago town of Ettrick. That was only a month before he was to kill Kylie and part of his bail conditions were that he reside in Ettrick, not in Owaka.

"The day we lost Kylie, Bailey was working in the community for different people, all organised by the Baptist Church," said Bevan Smith. "They even helped him get a vehicle and accommodation in an old house not far from Owaka."

Not long after Kylie died the Smiths learnt that Bailey was living locally because of a "problem" he had in Central Otago. With a sense of urgency to find out why Bailey killed his only daughter, Bevan Smith went through to Alexandra and began digging for information. From there he went to Ettrick and Dunedin, speaking to police, court officials, solicitors and Bailey's previous employer. What he found out made him angrier and angrier. Angry at a justice system that let Bailey loose in a community where few people knew either of him or about him.

"How can you protect people from the likes of Bailey if no one tells you what he's been up to?"

In Owaka some members of the Baptist Church knew Bailey had been arrested on a serious charge but others were ignorant of his goings-on. Some naively believed what they were told, that Bailey was being looked after by the church because he got into trouble in Central – he patted a woman's backside in a hotel! No. Bailey had been arrested and bailed after attempting to rape a woman, this was a serious attempted rape in that he used a knife to commit the offence. While the fact he was allowed bail at all did nothing to calm Bevan Smith's anger, the ease with which he could breach the bail conditions made him furious.

"For a start he was on a curfew from 7.00pm to 7.00am and this was extended to 10.00pm so he could work in an orchard," Bevan Smith said. "At the time of the bail application he didn't even have a job."

Bevan Smith spoke to Bailey's previous employer who said that he had evicted Bailey the night of the attempted rape. While Bailey's de facto wife and three children could remain in the rented house, Bailey had to go. At the time of the bail application Bailey was no longer living in Ettrick yet the bail conditions were that he live in the house he occupied at the time he was evicted. Bailey, who was said to have a drinking problem was to also abstain from liquor. Bevan Smith became frustrated.

"I tackled Bailey's defence counsel about the bail conditions and he said he could only convey to the judge what the client tells him," Bevan said.

Bevan Smith is an even-tempered man. He is measured in what he says and speaks clearly and deliberately. He is neither emotive nor sensational. But his frustration shows when he talks of the sloppy system of keeping track of serious criminal offenders.

"If Bailey had a problem, who was going to keep a check on him?" Bevan Smith went on to say. "The local police in Roxburgh and Alexandra had to personally talk to all of the hoteliers to say not to serve Bailey. But who would know him if he went into a hotel anyway? Then he was to reside at a place he never even lived at." Bevan Smith believes the system is irresponsible with few, if any, checks and balances.

"When applying for bail a solicitor should, if he is making the application, be sure himself that the facts are right," Bevan Smith claims. Bevan's bitterness even extended to Bailey's defence counsel in Alexandra.

"When I spoke to him, after I had introduced myself, he said something I could hardly believe," said an incredulous Smith. "He claimed that when he heard there was a young girl missing in Owaka he had a sick feeling inside." He knew what Bailey was like, yet got him those bail conditions without even a reporting clause.

If Bevan Smith was angry and frustrated at the "system" it was nothing compared to what he felt for the members of the Baptist Church. Had Bailey been made to fulfil the conditions, the locals at Roxburgh could have kept an eye on him. But soon after the bail conditions were set and supposedly began, members of the Owaka Baptist Church went through to Central Otago and helped Bailey move to Owaka. Never mind the fact he was to reside in a particular place, it seemed that they, the church, could look after Bailey and so they arranged Owaka to be his safe haven.

Until he got a car, Bailey was restricted. He was reported as having stayed around his house and occasionally cutting the hedges and tidying up. But, when they helped him find a car, he was free at last. No reporting clauses, no restrictions to liquor, nothing! Even the local constable was unaware of Bailey's background. Had he known he would have been very, very concerned. It was bad enough that Bailey was on bail for a serious sexual assault, but his background, established weeks after his arrest for Kylie's murder, prompted the detective investigating Bailey to say what she thought of him. She claimed that Paul David Bailey would be one of the most perverted offenders she's ever dealt with or made enquiries about. Furthermore, Bailey had sexual fetishes for young, attractive schoolgirls.

Apart from a few selected church elders, no one knew that among them was a dangerous sexual deviant who was soon to select a target, a quality target, and subject her to the most terrifying and degrading ordeal possible.

For some time it was feared Bailey was searching for his target. But only in hindsight would people realise how sinister his movements were. Bailey had bought a blue Volkswagen car which became quite distinctive. He had been seen around the town following the school bus. He also parked it outside Kylie's grandparents' house only a couple of hundred metres from the Catlins School. Several afternoons each week Kylie would visit her grandparents to have lunch together. At one stage Bailey had approached Kylie while she was riding with her friend but she had just said to ignore him and keep riding. Had she thought to mention it to her parents it is unlikely to have made much difference. No one knew of Bailey and any casual approaches he might have made would have seemed less sinister than they were. At one stage he followed another girl who, like Kylie, had long blond hair. It seems certain that Bailey was intent on a rape and 1 November, 1991 was the day he put his thoughts into action.

From the police summary read in court it was clear Bailey's intentions were set from the time he got out of bed that morning. The following is part of the police summary read to the court after Bailey pleaded guilty to the killing of Kylie Smith:

Crown Prosecutor Mr Bill Wright told the court Bailey drove to Balclutha from his Kaka Point address to Balclutha Motors where he asked for a map of the Owaka area, in particular one detailing gravel roads. He returned to Kaka Point and about 2pm loaded his .22 calibre, cut down semi-automatic rifle. Bailey did not have a firearm's licence. His de facto wife asked Bailey why he took the gun and was told he was going to finish drainage work and took the gun in case he saw any rabbits. Bailey then drove to Owaka and Pounawea, completed a slow circuit of the town in his blue Volkswagen vehicle, stopping at the telephone box for several minutes. He then drove back to Owaka where he noticed a 17-year-old girl walking along Waikawa Road. Bailey turned his vehicle and drove slowly past the girl, staring at her. He then proceeded to Catlins Area School where he entered the grounds and was seen acting suspiciously behind a hedge and was confronted by a teacher. Bailey then drove around Owaka and parked on the corner of Stuart Street and Main Road. The court was told Kylie had decided to ride her horse Nick after school, a normal routine. She wore a threequarter length riding coat, helmet, boots and carried a crop. She rode past Bailey who had been observing her and witnesses said he looked nervous and was reading a map while in the car. The accused then started his car, drove past Kylie and parked at the left hand side of the road. He caught Kylie's attention, they talked and according to the police reconstruction Bailey then produced the rifle and forced her into his car. They left the area and Owaka residents were alerted when the horse returned riderless. At approximately 4.45pm Bailey was driving north from Owaka at speed when he veered into the path of an oncoming vehicle, forcing it into a ditch. Police believe Kylie was huddled in the car at the time. Bailey then drove to the war memorial turnoff on Ahuriri Road and drove along Karora Creek Road, turning right towards Nugget Point. He was still travelling at speed and rounded a corner, colliding head on with two American tourists travelling in a Toyota vehicle. He reversed and drove towards the lighthouse. Both tourists stated Bailey was the only occupant visible in the car but police believe Kylie was still huddled in the vehicle at gunpoint. Bailey then returned to the Karora Creek Road and drove 1.2 kilometres where he came to an area known locally as Painted Rock. The court was told that Bailey had been seen at this location the previous night. Kylie was ordered from the vehicle, forced to walk across a stream and through thick bush at gunpoint. Both walked a further 150 metres into dense bush to a depression about 2 metres in diameter. Kylie was forced to remove her clothing and Bailey sexually violated her. He then allowed her to re-dress but before she was fully clothed he shot her in the back of the head. Kylie fell forward with her upper body facing downhill. Bailey dragged her into a depression and shot her twice more above the left ear. He placed her riding coat over her body, put the helmet and crop beside her and covered the area with foliage. The autopsy report stated there were numerous abrasions and cuts to Kylie's body. Bailey left the area approximately 6.45-7.00pm and drove to Kaka Point where he concealed the rifle in lupins and drove home about 7.15pm. Kylie had been detained by Bailey for more than 2 hours and had travelled approximately 30 kilometres during the ordeal. Bailey was approached by police at his house that night and denied any association with Kylie, stating he had been looking for work when he forced the vehicle from the road and that he had driven to view the penguins when he collided with the tourists at Nugget Point. The court was told Bailey and his partner said prayers for the Smith family that night. The next day Bailey continued to deny involvement with Kylie when questioned. When told the body had been found and after seeking legal advice, he refused to answer further questions.

After the summary had been read to court Bailey was convicted and remanded in custody to appear in the Dunedin district court at noon that same day. When he appeared for sentence accompanied by two prison guards he continued to show little emotion and was sentenced to 13 years on the rape charge and life imprisonment for the murder of Kylie Smith.

The first anyone knew of Kylie's abduction had been signalled when Nick, her riderless horse, was seen trotting home. Almost immediately Bevan Smith knew something serious was wrong.

"Nick was a calm horse," he said, "and Kylie was too competent a rider to fall." Still hoping that his daughter had fallen, Bevan made a quick search before sounding the siren at Owaka's tiny fire station. Dawn Smith was at the school, comforting a younger teacher who had been made redundant that day. Like Bevan, Dawn had a sinking premonition something dreadful had happened.

"When her horse came back alone," Dawn Smith said in a hardly audible whisper, "I had this terrible, terrible fear."

Despite the fears of the Smiths they couldn't comprehend the terrible fate their only daughter was suffering at the very time locals turned out and began searching. It was at this time that people's true colours showed. Not only did the locals turn out in force to help but so too did young people from Dunedin. Rhiane Smith, then only a 17-year-old boarding at Otago Boys' High School, was a popular young man. Throughout the Friday night five or six carloads of students appeared at the Smiths, all prepared to join the search for Rhiane's missing sister. It was those kinds of gestures that Bevan and Dawn remember, that and the support of friends and family.

The death of Kylie has had a huge impact on the Smiths, on Owaka and New Zealand. Following a funeral service and burial at the Owaka cemetery the pain for Bevan and Dawn has not diminished. They believe that Kylie's death need not have happened. And they believe that the justice system in "God's Own" is not what the people want. They believe, as do hundreds of thousands of New Zealanders that for a rape and murder as brutal and calculated as that perpetrated by Bailey the sentences are inadequate. Only when positive action is taken can they, and others at Owaka rest. The pain of Kylie's loss will be felt forever but her death must not be in vain. Two years after Kylie was taken the Smiths were as determined as ever, if not more so, that the balance must be redressed.

While Bevan is bitter about the involvement of the Baptist Church in this whole sorry saga that is not what haunts him.

"Sure I'm bitter," he said, his wife Dawn nodding in agreement. "I just couldn't face the members of the church," he said. "I'd probably flatten them."

Bevan Smith is adamant that no matter what those responsible for relocating Bailey did, they believed they were doing it for the right reasons. "But they won't admit that they made a mistake," he said.

Both he and his wife believe that the church members still think they had complete justification in having Bailey in Owaka. Dawn Smith is even more pointed.

"One of the church women said Bailey killed Kylie because he was possessed by the devil," said a disbelieving Dawn. "They not only set out to help him but one of the women told me they would 'fix him of his problem'."

Bailey's attack on Kylie came just one month after he was bailed for attempting to rape a woman at knifepoint. Those are the frustrations the Smiths live with but it doesn't compare to their thoughts of rights and justice. Justice for whom they ponder?

What haunts Bevan Smith is the realisation that 10 years after he killed Kylie, Paul David Bailey could be freed. Bevan is not an outwardly violent or vindictive man but his resolve is clear. He believes that there is not enough room in New Zealand for himself and the man who so callously murdered his daughter.

"Kylie would have been frightened," he said, almost disbelievingly, "she would have been frightened something terrible."

And that's why the thought of Bailey ever being freed haunts him. To the minds of the Smiths the man deserves no rights again.

About that time a woman, known only occasionally to the Smiths, visited them.

"What can I do to help?" Debbie Francis asked them. "I'll even walk to Wellington if it will help," she said.

That very night the idea of presenting a petition to Parliament for harsher sentences was born. Not out of vindication or hatred, but to ensure that people like Paul Bailey paid the price for premeditated murder. They wanted life for life and to tighten up bail conditions for sexual offenders. They weren't alone in their beliefs. In the same month that they presented their petition it was reported that the Police Complaints Authority, former High Court judge Sir John Jeffries, his former colleague Sir Clinton Roper and the now late Mike Bungay QC, one of New Zealand's foremost criminal lawyers, supported a new method of categorising murder. The type of crime committed on

Kylie Smith was at the uppermost range of the scale of degrading human behaviour.

Debbie Francis' entry into the arena became a godsend for Bevan and Dawn Smith.

"At least it gave us an opportunity to talk about Kylie," Dawn said with obvious relief. "It is so very easy to have your own thoughts but to mention her name often made others uncomfortable."

Dawn now makes a point of talking about Kylie often. Especially at school and for that first year she, and Bevan, found Debbie and others to be a real comfort.

When a tragedy on a scale of Kylie's killing happens there are many other side issues and problems to deal with. The media fighting over stories has to be faced and dealt with. The Smiths found many of the journalists excellent but they were not spared the clamour as the media competed for the scoop or the exclusive.

One of Bailey's two defence counsel was a local man who had even played rugby against Bevan Smith. Yet Bevan just could not rationalise how a local man, part of the community, could actually defend and try to have freed a man like Bailey.

"I was told that he was duty bound to defend Bailey whether he liked it or not," Bevan said. He doesn't believe that for a moment. "Surely he could say he shouldn't for personal reasons," said a man who was hurt by the solicitor's decision.

A common thread in many murders is the unnecessary but hurtful gossip. In a small community like Owaka any loose talk is sure to get back to someone. Loose talk was not a major problem for the Smiths, but enough was said to add to the pain.

"Sometimes I wonder when it will stop," said Dawn Smith, realising she has already been through enough. "Silly gossip and the church people with their self-righteousness can be hard to take," she said. "It seems crazy, but our movements to the cemetery are even monitored by one or two small-minded people. We either go too often or not enough, it's just stupid thinking," she said. "Others said the petition divided our community which we just don't believe," Dawn said with a touch of disappointment in her voice. "Sure, some find it hard to cope, but I think there is a touch of jealousy there," she added. "If only they knew, we don't want the publicity and never have, we just want justice but it won't happen on its own."

Bevan was able to sum up his thoughts regarding those who are prone to gossip or make inappropriate comments.

"I would dearly love to have Kylie back and for the ones Dawn's talking about to sacrifice one of their children," Bevan said, obviously knowing just how much Kylie's loss has meant to his wife. "I'd dearly love to swap places," he said, and he means it.

Both Bevan and Dawn are by nature quiet people who don't want the lights of publicity. But through the action of Paul Bailey the glare of publicity settled on the tiny township of Owaka and the Smiths in particular. There is no getting away from it. It wasn't their choice but there is no way either Bevan or Dawn Smith will let the loss of Kylie go for nothing. They realise now just how many of their fellow New Zealanders are hurting by a system designed to help and protect the perpetrators of crime. And they are not about to rest until the concerns of others are addressed.

Dawn in particular is learning to cope without Kylie and it's very, very difficult. "We've been told we should be getting over it by now," said Dawn almost incredulously. "That was said to us after only 18 months, almost as if you turn a grieving tap off after a certain time. Well you can't," Dawn Smith continued. "I still ponder at why Bailey chose Kylie. She was an attractive girl with a bubbly personality and had everything going for her. And, Kylie wasn't the perfect child, there's no such thing, but she was pretty damned close to it."

The Smiths can talk about Kylie and of the man who murdered her. For the first few months even that was denied them as they waited for the court case. There was just no way they would want to jeopardise the pending court case by making comments and Bevan Smith found that very difficult but now it doesn't matter and the petition begun in Owaka to redress the balance between victims and offenders is something he believes in. For Bevan and Dawn Smith along with their son Rhiane, one of New Zealand's more promising young cricketers, it is now a matter of getting on with their lives as so many other friends and family of murder victims have to. But it won't take away the pain of the loss or the haunting visions of Kylie's ordeal.

Owaka is the gateway of the beautiful Catlins Area, one of New Zealand's best kept secrets. The tranquil beauty of the area resplendent with its abundance of wildlife is a popular stopover for tourists. But Owaka won't be remembered for that. Bevan and Dawn Smith have taken great pride in watching Rhiane play first class cricket for Otago at the age of 18. His all-round talent is already being harnessed by Nottinghamshire and hopefully he will go on to higher cricketing honours. Kylie promised to be an equestrian of immense talent but that has now gone. Instead of Owaka being synonymous with tranquillity and success it seems it will be remembered more for tragedy and sorrow. And it was all so unnecessary.

Only three years after being sentenced for this shocking crime, Paul Bailey was in a minimum security prison in Christchurch.

3

Nora Emma Sole

Early in the evening of 7 February, 1992, 83-year-old Nora Sole went to bed. During the night a man broke into the elderly widow's house and, after beating her, tied her to the bed, raped and smothered her until she died. This was a particularly brutal murder of a defenceless old lady in her own home.

Perhaps apart from the killing of children, there can be no crime more revolting than the rape and murder of an elderly, defenceless woman in her own home.

Such a dreadful crime happened during the night of 7 February 1992. Eighty-three-year-old Nora Sole was an active woman for her age. Keen on bowls and playing cards she not only drove her own car but visited and helped other elderly folk less mobile than herself. Nora was a determined lady who did everything around her home except cutting the lawns and hedges and any heavy pruning.

On the fateful day a group of 10 elderly lady companions shared a birthday lunch together with Nora in one of their homes. About 5pm Nora dropped one of her friends home before returning to her New Plymouth house. Neighbours saw Mrs Sole inside before night fell but that was the last time this generous old lady was seen alive.

At some stage during that night someone broke in to what should have been Nora's sanctuary. After battering her he tied her to the bed, raped and then smothered this innocent harmless individual. After smoking a marijuana cigarette the offender went outside, searched Nora's car and tried to remove what evidence he could. Perhaps the arrival home of a next door neighbour panicked the man into action as he then tried to set fire to the house. A sheepskin rug in which the fire was set probably stopped the flames spreading and eventually the fire petered out.

The following morning, at around 11am, a neighbour found the elderly lady dead and after gently covering her rang the police.

Nora Sole had four children but this is the story of one, her 53-year-old bachelor son Perry. The affect this crime had on him was profound and this is the account of the son who had to endure the torment of a loved mother murdered in a hideous way.

Saturday, 8 February 1992 began as an ordinary sort of day. I was at the nursery where I was a manager having a light lunch in our office. Our sales reps from the United Kingdom and USA were with us when I got a phone call from my brother-in-law. He told me Mum had died and that I should come home immediately. I went into a sort of shock as, although Mum was 83, her death was quite unexpected. Only two days earlier I had been pruning fruit trees for her. She was quite bubbly and excited about a bowling trip to North Auckland two weeks later and about a Malvina Major concert she and friends were booked to see on the weekend. Even so, I sat down and finished the sandwich before calmly telling the others Mum had died and that I would have to go.

When I got to Mum's my sister Pam was there with her husband and two young policemen. I was rather puzzled that they were waiting outside. Pam had been in the house and identified Mum but when I arrived I was told to wait outside. As we waited Pam told me of burnt papers between the beds and curry powder spread along the hallway. We could see a broken table under a window which had obviously been forced open and we began to try convincing ourselves that a burglar had got inside and Mum, on being confronted, had suffered a heart attack. Well, that was the scenario we wanted to believe, anything else would have seemed unthinkable.

With nothing else to do we left and went to Pam's with other family members. Soon children, grandchildren and others were all together in New Plymouth and as the night wore on we tried to push thoughts away, but it was impossible. I remember getting up at four in the morning and having a cup of tea with Pam and when she said she wanted to talk to Victim Support it was obvious she knew or suspected more than she was saying.

After spending most of the morning contacting friends and telling them not to worry as Mum probably had a heart attack on seeing an intruder we began thinking of funeral arrangements. But at 5pm that night the police called a family conference. To our surprise they had post mortem results. That's when one poor fellow had the task of telling us what had happened. That our elderly mother had been raped and smothered. Some of the family cried, others cursed except Pam who must have known all along as she sat wooden and silent at the news. I too had guessed the worst and like Pam went cold and quiet. Very quickly the gathering broke up as we all needed to be with our thoughts.

Nora Emma Sole.

Unable to face the family and not wanting to go to an empty home I visited friends and only then found the events too much and broke down. Concern and kindness from friends seemed to upset me more than anything else and that's the way it was for a long time. It's amazing how, in times like this, people stick by you. Some of my friends offered such tremendous support and encouragement and I've often wondered, if roles were reversed, if I would have offered them the same kind of help.

Where friends and family spoke openly and honestly about Mum's loss and the ongoing investigation looking for her killer, others became very aloof. People who previously spoke to me at work suddenly became too busy to talk. Others might say hello Perry then whoosh, were gone. This was a difficult period for me and no doubt is for many people in my predicament. Some acquaintances cope well when talking to someone who has suffered such a publicised loss. Others just can't cope and it's not only obvious but makes one very sensitive to other people's attitudes.

I soon began to get an obsession with law and order and in that frame of mind it is almost impossible to concentrate on work. When working alone in fields at the nursery my mind would wander on to a track that left me depressed and often in tears. Looking back I would have agreed with my employers had I been dismissed. Over those first six months following Mum's murder I certainly didn't feel as if I earned my salary.

Soon after Mum's funeral I sought help through Victim Support and was put on to a volunteer who helped me in the early stages, but the misery I felt lasted a lot longer than he led me to expect. I never resigned as a manager of the nursery at first as I expected to "come right" at any time, but experience shows you don't suddenly get over things. Depending on a person's nature and circumstances leading up to their grief it's obvious that we all react differently. One thing is for sure though, when you lose a close relative or friend in a tragic way such as we lost our mother, the trauma is very pronounced and lasting.

Attitudes in the social sense were similar to work. It took some people months to talk to me while others moved away very quickly. I don't really blame them, it is understandably difficult to talk to someone who's had a loss. What do you say? But for the sufferer it's more difficult being avoided than openly talking about what's happened.

It's so easy to just stay home and become a hermit but that's not the way it should be. I often thought, "What the hell, they have to get used to the idea that I'm here to stay and I'm not going to disappear to suit them."

At the golf club or workingmen's club life goes on and I knew I had to go sooner or later. In retrospect I probably got "back into it" a bit quicker than perhaps I should. With an obvious case of butterflies I went to the workingmen's club, got myself a beer and went up to my usual group. I was greeted with a shocked silence and found myself completely tongue-tied. In the main it was me approaching others, not them me. The golf club was different and if I was approached the nervousness went. It's a strange sensation being in a position where friends can't talk to you about something like Mum's murder, knowing that the situation made them uneasy. But you cannot live in a vacuum, you have to get back to as normal a life as possible.

If I had to do this all over again, I'd certainly do some things differently. Two months after Mum's murder I heard of an elderly woman's death on the morning news. She was 83, the same age as Mum. I had had little sleep over the past eight weeks and coupled with the constant tension I'd just reached breaking point. During the 15 kilometres drive to work that morning I had to pull off the road and just broke down. The same thing happened later that morning at work.

A break away was essential and two nights with my sister at Kawakawa Bay and four nights with friends on Auckland's North Shore was just what I needed. Apart from one phone call from the police I was able to get away from it all. During this trip north I learned of Odette Leather* who had an action group in Auckland. Attending a meeting I found members of her group to be real lifesavers. They offered the sort of contact I needed, having had similar experiences. Not everyone needs that contact but I did.

The obsession with law and order was still with me. I simply couldn't get my mind off it. This was prior to an arrest being made for Mum's murder and a feeling of helplessness and of being useless crept in. There was nothing physical we could do, and at times were not even able to answer police questions.

For weeks we were unable to enter Mum's home unless police were present. With fruit rotting and food in the fridge going off we had to go in with a police escort. A whole month passed before we could sort out Mum's effects and even then the smell from the fire was still obvious.

The police asked us to do two interviews with television and other media. No one in the family either wanted to do the interviews or have the media in our homes so the first was done in the police canteen. My initial reaction on seeing the television cameras being set up was to start shaking. Thankfully the interviewers were human and not my preconceived idea of hardened, aggressive professionals. It was still a nerving experience.

Ten weeks had now passed since Mum's death. Throughout that time we were in a state of tension. Poor sleeping patterns, waiting for results that never came, lack of concentration and the nervousness at meeting people were constant companions. Throughout that time recurring thoughts were always there. Why did it happen? Why Mum?

41

We believed that it just didn't happen in families like ours.

About two months after the tragic night a senior policeman from Palmerston North came to review the file, checking every detail in case something hadn't been told to them. Because I had never married I was even asked if I was homosexual and at that point I believed they had come to a stop in their enquiries. Now they were looking for new angles as other avenues of enquiry were exhausted.

A breakthrough came at the same time. A letterbox drop of pamphlets was made seeking information and that is when the desired result was made. On an afternoon I had arrived back from Auckland we were told an arrest would be made that day and we were to be at a debriefing at 5pm. Initially our excitement was great but by 5pm it was wearing thin. After hearing details and background of the guy who raped and smothered our elderly mother it just set up the questions again. Why? And why our mother?

We still don't know and may never know the answers. One of my nieces had a bottle of wine she swore to open to celebrate the arrest. Strangely I didn't want to celebrate. Although we were relieved the murderer was now caught it just didn't give us the lift we thought it might. Nothing had really changed. After a short while the "celebrations" broke up.

When the police made their letterbox drop seeking help from the public a local talkback radio host had criticised the police for "abusing their powers". I was livid and though it might seem petty now I refused that radio station any comments after the arrest.

I've got little faith in the ACC or justice system as it relates to victims. ACC made an automatic payment which amounted to about half the funeral expenses. Being such an unnatural death the service was larger than we might have expected had Mum just passed away. There was a lot of concern shown by many people and we spent $700 alone on thank you cards and postage replying to the many well wishers.

I alone lost over $5,000 in salary in the first 15 months. That's not counting sick leave and holidays spent "on the case, and its effects". All my working life I've paid taxes in part supporting people in need and even in the defence of criminals on legal aid. For the first time in my life I am struggling, all due to the criminal acts of someone else, both Justice and ACC say in effect, "Go to hell, we have no money for people like you."

From the time I put in a claim with ACC, I was encouraged by letter and phone to withdraw it. Information from them was slow and the chances of compensation nil. I believe something has to be done. There has to be some way of recovering direct losses. It's not our fault that someone broke into Mum's home and took her life. It seems that the rights of an offender and the rights of a family are inequitable.

And of the trial? We found the High Court trial most dissatisfying. Because of our system of justice the murderer never had to speak and admit what he did even when he eventually pleaded guilty. Everything was over in 10 minutes leaving us feeling nothing had changed and that nothing had even happened. It took weeks to get over our empty feeling and acknowledge that at last the saga was ended. Of course we were relieved. Relieved that all the gruesome details didn't have to be made public but we also felt badly let down. It might seem a strange inconsistency to feel let down after your mother's murderer pleads guilty and is sentenced to life in prison, but in reality the justice system is a game, a legal game for lawyers and too often the victims and the public are the losers.

Two weeks prior to the first scheduled trial there was a postponement. Dates had to be rescheduled. A second postponement came just 10 days in advance, as the murderer's defence counsel from Palmerston North had another case in Wanganui. Was our family's welfare ever considered or was our opinion ever sought? Not likely. Only the defence requirements. It seems that was all that mattered.

A lawyer has since told me we were lucky our case didn't go through the High Court. When there is nothing to lose they usually "give it a go". See, it's a game. In other words truth, justice and morals don't matter.

From my experience following this tragedy six things became obvious. Firstly there is a subconscious mind that protects your body. It takes us a long long time to realise what is happening to us. Secondly the family stayed close and supportive. We all had to find ways of coping which are different yet we still had to worry about each other. I think our greatest fear was of family arguments and splits so we all had to work hard to avoid those things happening. Thirdly I no longer respect the justice system. The system and some lawyers have only earned my contempt. I marvel at the way some can live with themselves. Next, my realisation that throughout this tragic episode representatives of government departments and religions were noticeable by their absence.

My whole outlook on life was slowly but surely changing. I now have a shorter temper. I have a stubborn, fighting spirit I never realised I owned. Unlike the past, previously important things no longer matter very much but my compassion for victims is strong.

This article was written in October 1993, eighteen months after Mum's murder. Now, a further two years on some things have changed. The ACC have finally settled the claim though it took two years from the time it was lodged. Although my attitudes and beliefs have continued to change a general unsettled feeling remains. Little things still happen reminding one of the event, keeping the emotions stirred up. The headaches however, that used to be a regular feature now occur only occasionally.

And finally some friends and acquaintances will never realise how much they have helped, whilst others who tried to help were never given the chance due to my nervousness at getting into new situations. Other people just don't understand, and I used to be one of them.

Odette Leather, who gave so much help to Perry Sole and others, died in Middlemore Hospital during the writing of this book. In 1985 Odette formed the lobby group Citizens Against Violence and became a lifeline to many families of murder victims. She also fought hard to get compensation from ACC for those families.

4

Craig Merryweather

When Craig Merryweather went 'missing' on 17 August 1987, it began over two years of anguish and uncertainty for his parents. After meeting three young men in Picton, Craig accepted a lift to his intended destination on the southern skifields. Intent on robbery, the three killed Craig, burying him near the Lindis Pass. Following a Crimewatch programme, Craig's body was recovered and the three were arrested.

When Craig went missing his parents *knew* something was wrong. And the fact he was 'missing' made the situation for David and Beth Merryweather of Ramarama, south of Auckland, all the more difficult. As if the trauma of a murder investigation and subsequent trials are not enough to cope with, having their son missing for over two years before knowing his fate compounds the situation greatly.

The parents of Craig Merryweather, who had to suffer such an ordeal explain the situation as they see it. The events leading up to Craig's untimely death, the anguish they faced, their views on crime and punishment and the development of an unexpectedly unique friendship follows...

The last time we heard directly from Craig was on the afternoon of 16 August 1987. At the time we had a bit of a laugh. Richard, the eldest son of close friends in Wellington arrived out of the blue on this brilliantly fine afternoon. While talking to Richard, Craig rang from Richard's parents' house in Wellington. Of course there were comments about swapping eldest sons. We were surprised to hear he was in Wellington as we thought he was at Mount Ruapehu, at the Massey Alpine Club Hut, skiing. It transpired that with very little snow at Ruapehu he decided to journey south to Queenstown where there was ample snow and excellent conditions. Ironically, two weeks later there was so much snow at Ruapehu that the North Island Championships were cancelled. Craig had hitched a lift from Palmerston North, where he was a student at Massey University, to Wellington. He had time to spare before the evening sailing of the inter-island ferry so had spent the afternoon with our Wellington friends before boarding the ferry that evening. This was the last confirmed sighting we had.

The next happening was a phone call from the Picton police to us late on the afternoon of 18 August. We were told a lot of clothing and ski equipment had been found thrown over a bank on Queen Charlotte Drive overlooking the port of Picton. Amongst the gear was Craig's student ID card and driver's licence which is how the police traced its ownership. Immediately the alarm bells sounded, but as the police told us theft was rife on the ferries we fully expected a collect phone call from Craig asking for financial help to find his way home. Nothing was heard and although worried, we consoled ourselves that someone as self-sufficient as Craig probably thought that even though his gear was gone, he would make the best of it and amble around with what he had on his back. Furthermore, there were transactions on his bankcard with withdrawals from his account. Craig was an experienced tramper who could literally live on very little and if necessary make what he had go a long way. The police were extremely sympathetic but pointed out that a person does not become missing unless at least a week overdue from their expected date of return, so nothing could be done until this period of time had elapsed.

We *knew* something was wrong as our son would not have simply gone off like this without telling us. If it had been a girl there would have been a marked outcry because of the sex aspect, but as the police said there was absolutely no motive for murdering a male student. Of the alternatives, accident, suicide, murder or deliberate disappearance, murder was the last on the list. Deliberate disappearance was their pick as it is apparently quite common in young people of that age group. We strongly disagreed. They did not know our son. It was completely out of character.

The police were surprised we had flown to Picton in order to search for Craig as it was their experience that a lot of parents could not care less about their children, and we hope that this obviously caring attitude might have influenced them in their liaison with the Crimewatch people at a later date.

We placed advertisements and a photo in every daily newspaper in New Zealand. The story was picked up by other news media and Independent Radio News in particular gave it wide coverage. A friend on a business trip said it followed him right around the South Island. This cost thousands but we did not care as we would do

Craig Merryweather.

anything in order to find our son. We had many responses to the advertisements, all from people who were really sympathetic to our plight, but there were no positive sightings. Craig was distinctive in that he was very tall, about 6 foot 5 inches and unlike a lot of very tall people held himself erect which made the most of his height. Because of this he stood out in the crowd. Absolutely nothing was heard. It was as if the earth had swallowed him up. The police did their best but there was absolutely nothing to go on.

We then had the traumatic task of cleaning out his flat in Palmerston North and bringing all the possessions home. Plans for his 21st birthday which was to have been 25 October were shelved and the clothes from Picton were recovered. This state of limbo lasted for two and a quarter years with nothing heard. His room was ready for him with all his university paraphernalia awaiting the return. The champagne bought for the 21st was carefully stored in the hopes of an eventual celebration and we were unable to touch this until 1995, so affected were we by the association.

In October 1989 we were approached by Gilly Tierney, then producer of the Crimewatch programme who were doing a programme on missing persons and asked if we would be willing to feature Craig as one of those missing. Nothing ventured, nothing gained, so although we are a private family we agreed to feature in it. We did not hold out high hopes but were willing to try anything. Crimewatch had featured his case in a short snippet at the time of the disappearance, but on this occasion they were making a feature of it, with a reconstruction of his boarding the ferry etc. We were impressed by two features of the production team: their professionalism and extreme youth. We both felt positively geriatric.

On the night of the programme the police officer presenting it said they had had quite a few calls but for us not to get our hopes up. On the following Monday we had a phone call from Detective Grant Nicholls of the Palmerston North police who wanted to talk over the case with us. He would not disclose any details over the phone so we thought he was coming up on routine business and would just confirm there had been no result from the Crimewatch programme. On his arrival we thought something was amiss when he sent his driver away and said he would be with us for quite a while. Soon after he broke the news that they were positive Craig's body would be found and that he had been murdered. This absolutely devastated us as although we always feared the worst we had always hoped for the best. It was, and still is, absolutely inconceivable to us that anyone could deliberately and callously murder a fine clean-living young man with so much to offer the world.

Detective Nicholls had an item of Craig's clothing that Beth was able to identify and he was with us all day amassing information. We were able to give him photos of Craig's pack and sleeping bag but he warned us not under any circumstances to let it be known that the police had a lead.

The following day was spent obtaining dental and medical records and checking on the pack and sleeping bag from Living Simply Ltd, the shop where they were purchased. The proprietor was extremely helpful and as luck would have it the South Island manufacturer's representative was visiting Auckland that day. The representative identified the pack from the photo and rang his employers Macpac, who immediately couriered an identical one to Palmerston North from their museum. All this was done in conditions of utmost secrecy.

The following weekend was Labour Weekend and we were due in

Wellington to celebrate the silver wedding of our close friends; the same ones who saw Craig off on the boat that fateful day. It was arranged we would call in to Palmerston North on the way down to check progress. As can be imagined we were absolutely screwed up on this journey and did not bother having the car radio on so were unaware of events happening in Palmerston North and relatives and friends knew before we did that Craig had definitely been murdered.

The first thing we saw as we pulled into the police yard was Detective Nicholls in a car with others just leaving. He jumped out and took us up to Detective Inspector Harry Hawthorn who broke the news that it was now positive that Craig had been murdered, and that three young men were 'assisting the police with their enquiries'. They were being flown to the Lindis Pass, the scene of the crime. We shed tears in abundance and even contemplated returning home. As we were in no condition to drive we stayed and had a good night's rest with sleeping pills prescribed by the police surgeon. As it happened we stayed for over a week to help as best we could. This was the most terrible period of time we have ever experienced.

It transpired the three suspects had been hit with a dawn raid the morning we were travelling south and several items of Craig's, including his pack and sleeping bag, were found in their possession. We were able to positively identify these items. About this time the news media had anticipated something was happening and were making their own enquiries. In order to forestall any false rumours, Detective Inspector Hawthorn made a full statement at midday of what was happening.

It seems that after Craig disembarked from the ferry he was walking up the road when asked by these three if he wanted a lift. This was just outside a backpacker's hostel and we are sure he was on the point of entering when they hailed him. Another 30 seconds and he would have been inside and they would have missed him. They were on the run from the police after jumping bail and wanted somebody to help pay for the petrol. They stopped that night at a Blenheim motor camp cabin and we are sure it was here they thought of the crime. Craig was everything they were not. Tall, handsome, well educated with an open contempt for cannabis smokers, which we believe they most certainly were. The following day they headed south where Craig bought petrol for them at a service station in Christchurch. He used the EftPos facility and one of them got his PIN number. Driving on, Craig was in the front seat and two sat behind him discussing, we believe, when and where they would murder him. They assumed that being a university student going skiing he would be loaded [they said as much in evidence] and as they had his PIN number they would be able to clean out his account which would have oodles of money in it. Anyone with half a brain would know students have no money and that if they did it would not be left in an account that did not pay interest. They were earning far more on the dole than Craig with his student bursary.

At the foot of the Lindis Pass, at Longslip Creek, they said the car was overheating and asked Craig to go down for some water. As he was walking away they shot him with a .22 rifle. He was not killed immediately so he was used for target practice, being shot several more times. The rifle was a single shot which necessitated reloading between shots, compounding the callous horror of their actions. They then dug a shallow grave and buried Craig while he was still breathing.

Of the killers, Duncan Mitchell did not actually pull the trigger but was still found guilty as a party to murder. The one who it is believed fired the first shot, Tony Wilkins, is an interesting character. Cold-blooded killing appears to mean nothing to him. At the time of his arrest for Craig's murder he was on bail while awaiting trial for a second murder. Sometime after killing Craig he had returned to Palmerston North and killed Grant Coldstream. It was said in evidence that after assassinating our son he slept like a baby and after stabbing Grant Coldstream he walked back to his accommodation, told his landlady, 'I've just killed some bloke ma,' and went upstairs and went to sleep. Before coming to trial he pleaded guilty to Craig's murder. This made no difference to his prison sentence as he was already serving a life sentence for Grant Coldstream's murder, and as you only have one life and he is already serving it, Craig's murder was in effect a 'freebie'.

The third of the trio, Jason Dermer, was at the time of his arrest for the murder, serving a sentence in prison so the police had no trouble in finding him. He must be a little more sensitive than appears as he apparently did his best to put Craig out of his misery. At the time of the murder none of the three were older than 17, so they may not even be 30 by the time they are released.

After the hasty burial they used Craig's card to buy petrol at Twizel and subsequently tried to withdraw funds at Picton. It was the use of the card that put us off the scent at the time. For all their efforts they got about $120.00. Before embarking on the ferry back to

Wellington, they threw a lot of Craig's gear over a bank above the town, keeping his good pack and sleeping bag and some clothing. At Paraparaumu they stayed with some people and they actually boasted of wasting a hitchhiker, but no one believed them, assuming the clothing to be obtained by theft. A coat of Craig's was given away and this was the item Beth was able to identify for Detective Nicholls.

Over two years later, on the night of the Crimewatch programme, the couple the trio had stayed with at Paraparaumu were arguing over which channel to watch and as they switched on the TV we appeared on the screen. The man commented, "I wonder if that has anything to do with Wilkins and Co?" She replied, "Well, there's a phone there, give them a ring." From that call the police had the lead they needed and the whole thing blew apart in a matter of days. As they said it was like riding a high speed roller coaster, things happened so fast they had no time to catch their breath.

From there the judicial process of preliminary hearing and trial followed. All the stress had exacerbated David's heart problems and at the time of the trial he was in Green Lane Hospital for a quadruple heart bypass operation. As soon as he could he went straight from the coronary ward to Palmerston North for the trial. Not the best convalescence after major surgery.

There were many peculiar happenings connected with this case. Some spring to mind. Shortly after Craig's disappearance we as Christians decided to hold a prayer vigil. This involved contacting as many of our friends as wanted to take part, and arranging for prayers to start at a specified time. This net was spread from Whangarei to Wellington. As farmers we of course have dogs, but one in particular, Cindy, a lovely golden labrador, was Craig's. On this night, just as the prayers were about to start at 7.30pm we heard Cindy barking outside. I said something rude and rushed outside as we did not want anybody disturbing us at this time. There was nobody there, so at the time I thought nothing of it. At 8.30pm when the prayers concluded she barked again, right on time. Again I went out but as before all was quiet. Talking about it later over a drink which was definitely stronger than tea, Beth and I realised that the first bark was not the alarm she gave if a stranger was around but the bark she gave when Craig hopped off the school bus and came down the drive. A distinctive short joyful yelp which usually preceded a yellow cannonball bolting up the drive in an endeavour to knock a schoolboy off his feet. It was uncanny that she barked the exact minute the prayers started and again the exact minute they finished.

At the trial one officer giving evidence stated that while at Lindis Pass he was sitting with Dermer, just chatting about nothing material when Dermer said, "When I saw this thing on that Crimewatch I knew we were f....d. I knew that you b.....s would get the stuff to find us even after this time."

The next was narrated to us by one of the police who was present at the scene of the crime. When the three were escorted by car from Queenstown to Lindis Pass they were taken individually to the scene of the crime. Two identified the scene and waved in the general direction of where the body lay but refused to go any nearer. Dermer however, as he was getting out of the car, felt as if he had been kicked, not pushed but definitely kicked in the small of the back. He whirled around thinking a policeman had assaulted him but there was nobody within 20 feet. He tried like the others to just gesture in the general direction of the grave but couldn't. He was pulled to the grave as if by a magnet and eventually came to a stop and pointed down to the site. He told the officer that he tried desperately to turn aside but had absolutely no show, and was completely incapable of doing so.

We argue at times over who did the actual kicking. My pick is a five-foot-one bundle of feisty Irish grandmother who exploded like dynamite if anything threatened her family. Beth on the other hand is adamant that it came from a tall iron-willed Lancashire grandmother who was equally protective of her own.

It is said that every cloud has a silver lining and as far as we are concerned the silver which came from this terrible affair is the unique friendship which has developed between ourselves and Kris and Ganga Aiyar. Their son Arjun had gone missing some years before Craig and were both featured on the same Crimewatch programme. They asked the TV people if, through them, they could contact us. The TV crew contacted us and when we said we would like to meet them, gave us the Aiyar's address.

While in Palmerston North with the investigations we met Kris and Ganga and immediately clicked. It was uncanny. They asked if they could come to Craig's funeral and this was only the second time we had met. While sitting in our bedroom afterwards, away from the crowd, the feeling was reinforced that we were closer to them than to many people we had known for years. It was almost as though we had been intensely close for a lifetime. Yet in a way we share nothing in common. We are Christian, they are Hindu. We are farmers, they are academics. We live in the country, they are townies. But the fact remains we have a relationship that transcends these differences. They supported us during the depositions hearing and the trial, always there when needed and giving us incredible comfort and strength to cope.

Thanks to Beth's insistence, Detective Nicholls [now detective senior sergeant] took up the case of their missing son Arjun, and had another look at it. He ferreted out some more relevant information and managed to get it featured on the Crimewatch programme again. On the night of the programme we were on our way to the South Island for a car club rally and stopped off overnight to be with Kris and Ganga to support them while watching Crimewatch. As in our case no one had any great hopes anything material would eventuate. We were to leave next morning but the ferry crews were on strike so we could not cross the strait. We stayed on that evening and while Kris and I went to buy some takeaways for dinner, Detective Nicholls and Detective Sergeant Denis O'Rourke arrived and told Ganga and Beth that Arjun's body had been found. Owing to the many years Arjun's body had lain in the bush it was impossible to establish the cause of death and the coroner returned an open verdict. Now it was our turn to help them when they were so distressed. We never did make the rally. For the next two weeks we stayed with Kris and Ganga and did the best we could to help.

Craig's body had been cremated soon after he was found and we were not aware until the trial that a portion of his skull was kept as vital forensic evidence. After the trial there remained the problem of what to do with this portion of Craig's body. It was too late to have it cremated with the rest of his remains and we wanted it treated with the same love and care as the rest of the body. We had asked the police to send it to Auckland and pending a decision by us it was left in the care of the undertaker.

On the only evening the four of us were alone, Beth suddenly asked Kris and Ganga if they would mind if this portion of Craig's body could be cremated with Arjun. We were overjoyed when they immediately agreed which left four grown adults crying their eyes out. We regard this as a further symbol of the strong links between us.

It has been said that there is no difference between a death by murder and accident or illness. Believe you me, there *is* a difference. It is a difference of intent. The sheer horror of knowing there are people capable of extinguishing a fine young man so callously and without pity for no real reason is beyond comprehension. The sheer depths of despair into which you plunge are beyond the worst imaginings, especially when during the trial it comes out in evidence that Craig was still breathing when buried. The anguish is compounded when one realises the killers will be released shortly, and resume life as normal. I also believe there is no remorse other than for being caught.

There have been calls lately for degrees of murder which have been studiously ignored. There is a considerable difference between the classic case of a man coming home unexpectedly and finding his wife in bed with the neighbour and committing what the French call the 'Crime Passionelle', and the brutal rape of a teenage girl or in our case, a cold-blooded execution. The crown prosecutor in Palmerston North, Mr Ben Vanderkolk, said he had prosecuted many murders and one execution and to us that is what Craig's murder was. The death penalty will never return but for brutal first degree murders the term should be for the whole of the murderer's natural life; no parole, no remission, nothing but the sight of bars for as long as he may live.

We firmly believe that violent criminals should fear retribution of the law and that consequences of offending should be clearly spelt out. Statistics show that violent crime is increasing at an horrendous rate, so the obvious conclusion must be: The soft option does not work. It has been tried and found wanting.

Where does one feel safer? Downtown Auckland with graffiti-spraying, glue-crazed street kids who will beat you up for fun knowing their likely punishment is weak, or Singapore where a minor infringement brings stern retribution? Japan is held up as a model law-abiding country, but those with experience of Japanese jails say that they are incredibly harsh.

It is said we have an extremely high imprisonment rate compared to most countries. The reason is simple: we have a higher crime rate. People who say prison is no deterrent and who quote the USA should reflect that we are not America, and that countries with harsher penalties are on the whole more law abiding than we are.

Most of the emphasis in the justice system is directed towards the offender. Legal aid, penal reform, rehabilitation; vast sums have been spent in the interests of hardened criminals with the poor victim of crime virtually forgotten. The ordinary law abiding taxpayer is ignored by the liberals who frame our laws and cannot see the obvious truth that as the severity of sentences has diminished the rate of crime, especially violent crime, has increased.

I am certainly not a qualified lawyer but believe in giving a first offender an even break. But all too many of these young people are repeat offenders who, as I said before, have no fear of the law because they have not received any real punishment from it.

They say that society gets the government it deserves. For too long grey people in grey offices in Wellington have inflicted their will on the public who have accepted it like sheep. In spite of the presentation of one of the largest petitions ever signed in this country it was virtually ignored by parliament. One wonders what planet some of these politicians inhabit. Unfortunately with the advent of MMP I feel things are only going to get worse. Issues of law and order are important to our future. Despite debates from academics we feel strongly that the soft option is clearly not working.

It is a peculiarity of this case that Craig Merryweather was killed on 17 August 1987, the day of the very first Crimewatch screening. That programme was to play a crucial role in discovering what happened to Craig. David and Beth were told of their son's fate on 17 October 1989 following the 17th Crimewatch programme. While it may not be of strong relevance to a lot of people the connection to Crimewatch and the number 17 is certainly relevant to the Merryweathers.

5

Craig Robertson

*In the evening of 16 March, 1991, Craig Robertson, aged 21,
left McDonald's restaurant in Hamilton and walked around a
car stopped on a pedestrian crossing. A passenger in the car had
earlier argued with others who objected to where the car was.
As Craig passed the car the passenger got out and struck him
across the bridge of the nose with what could have been a
wheelbrace, causing fatal injuries.*

Some time after Craig's death his mother Zeta was asked to write
about her experiences. The following are excerpts from her covering
letter to a counsellor and the collection of thoughts she penned. It
epitomises a mother's loss...

Dear Wendy
   Last night when you rang and I agreed to write something for you
about grief after murder, how much it hurts, how much pain, I really
thought it would be a breeze.
   It's 3pm now (yes, I have been putting it off, but I did have a couple
of things to deal with first). Craig had a computer disk for all his uni
assignments and I've been filling it up with my thoughts. His
assignments are still on it and I get heaps of pleasure from reading
them but then the "if onlys" start flooding in and the tears flow.

Craig Robertson and his sister Helen two months before his death.

However, I said "yes" to your request and hope that the enclosed might be of some use. At times such as last night when I was interviewed about my Lifeline course by *The Waikato Times*, I feel really strong. I believe I can offer support to others and picked up the phone and rang two good friends who have recently suffered as much. Jackie, whose husband was gunned down when he surprised intruders camping in his unoccupied farm house at Omori, and Pam, daughter of an 83-year-old who was raped and murdered in her New Plymouth home in February of this year. Then there are times when I feel too vulnerable to communicate with anyone.

I hope what I am about to write in the next hour or so is of some use to you. If I can help others in their grieving, surely I am helping myself too? By the way, I will always be grateful to you and Bruce for your contribution to my healing. It was at your course last May where I first heard of "A Grieving Process" and realised that perhaps I wasn't going mad after all. Regards to you both and keep up the good work.

The Grief After Murder – How Much It Hurts – How Much Pain: A Personal Opinion

The disbelief, the emptiness, the void, the desolation, the intense devastation is I guess similar to that experienced by any of us after the death of a loved one.

If the death is by natural causes, one can be grateful for the sufferer's release from pain.

If the death is a result of something over which the victim has control, such as a traffic accident involving speed/alcohol, or some suicides, the self-responsibility of the person involved has to be considered.

If the death is accidental, consolation that the victim knew nothing of what happened, can help.

But, in the case of murder, where somebody else has been responsible for a senseless and unnecessary, unprovoked attack resulting in the death of a loved one, the grief is intensified.

The one consoling feature of Craig's death was, according to the doctors at Waikato Hospital, that he would have been totally unaware of what had hit him. He would be deeply unconscious from that first 'round-house blow' from behind where the wheelbrace left its mark on the bridge of his nose. Then the crash to the pavement and the resultant brain damage sustained, factors of which he would have had no knowledge. Consolation indeed.

As well as having to cope with a tremendous loss, there was the uncertainty whether Craig had in fact antagonised his attacker or not. The police told us of two possible scenarios following statements taken from the offender and witnesses and although we were pretty sure that our gentle 21-year-old had done nothing wrong, it wasn't until six months later in the High Court that we were convinced Craig was totally innocent of any aggravation. And to think that I had given his killer the benefit of the doubt thinking that perhaps his story of just punching Craig was true, and that perhaps Craig had provoked the attack. No.

Our unfamiliarity with police and court proceedings only added to our distress. The police officer in charge of the case was very good about keeping us informed of progress in fixing a date for the trial. This kept changing because of another murder the month before Craig's, where one of the accused was to sit School Certificate.

The knowledge that Craig's murderer was entitled to legal aid with the best defence in the country, Mike Bungay QC no less, hurt considerably. Craig didn't even have an advocate and we were not allowed to have any communication with the crown prosecutor. The hurt intensified when the Judge, on his very first murder trial I believe, agreed with Mike Bungay that the accused, because he did not use a knife or a gun, did not intend to kill Craig. The lesser charge of manslaughter was brought to which the accused pleaded guilty. As I had met the trial judge's wife at a luncheon the week before and Mr Bungay could have claimed that because the Judge's wife knew the victim's mother, the sentence was too harsh, the accused was sentenced by another Judge: to three years in jail. We just couldn't believe that our beloved son's life was worth so little.

The crown prosecutor felt the sentence was a bit light but was unsuccessful in an appeal. The unfairness of the whole thing – what about self-responsibility?

The only thing Craig did wrong was to leave McDonald's Family Restaurant eating his second Kiwiburger and fries. He and four of his friends had already had a meal and left to get money from a money machine but Craig needed more food so he had gone back. When he was crossing the street to join his friends the accused got out of his car having already abused Craig's friends for touching the car he was a passenger in. The car was parked on a pedestrian crossing so people had to walk around it and when the accused believed Craig had bumped his car he got out, called to Craig, then hit him on the bridge of the nose causing fatal injuries.

The pain and the hurt seem never ending. Craig had a lot going for him. He was on track to have graduated BSc in May 1992 and could well have been overseas by now. He had lived at home and held part-time jobs at McDonald's and as a weight training gym instructor at the university recreation centre. These jobs helped him through his three year university course. His brother, older by 2 years, is at Massey doing his BAg and sister, 3 years younger than Craig, has a job in Auckland. Both miss him dreadfully. They were all such good mates, probably because they each went to different boarding schools and only saw each other during holidays through those traumatic teenage years, and hence appreciated each other more than happens in some families.

Craig's father and I will never get over the senselessness of his death. Some of us sit around waiting for things to happen. Craig made things happen. He was the one who lived life to the full. Just a month before he was murdered he went to Anakiwa for an Outward Bound course, a 21st birthday shout. When he first applied to Outward Bound they said they couldn't take him until November 1991 so he spent his birthday money doing courses in parachuting and scuba diving. We are so grateful now that he did get to Outward Bound when a vacancy occurred in the February course.

Just about every week we hear of senseless killings. Some penalties for violent crime are a lot harsher than that imposed on Craig's killer. The TV series Bungay on Crime does not help us in our grieving, but Richard and I are compelled to watch the programme. Maybe we are looking for a chink in his armour, or some proof of a theory I hold that the Judge was in fact intimidated by Mr Bungay.

Anniversaries are not easy. Craig's murder in March, his birthday six months later. It's now a year since the trial and last Friday a year since sentencing, just three years for our Craig's life.

I have a constant pain in the left side of my chest. After doing all sorts of tests my GP says it's heartache and I guess I'll have to live with it. Craig opted on his driving licence to be an organ donor. Three people have benefited with his heart and kidneys being used. More anguish for me when there was media coverage earlier in the year about the non-return of body parts to grieving relatives and the importance of burial of 'whole people'. I didn't need that.

I have been asking heaps of questions, searching for help, for reasons. I joined an Auckland Lifeline counselling course, "Surviving when someone you love was murdered." I have written to the crown prosecutor and the High Court and I have spent hours going through the judge's notes and the police file.

There is still an unanswered question: Why did the accused hit Craig?

My friendly detective sergeant assures me that people like him don't need reasons. If Craig had had any inkling that the man was behind him he could have defended himself. He was fit, he had done martial arts training.

Why was the car still on the pedestrian crossing for such a long time after Craig's friends had left the immediate area? I think I found the answer to that when going through the statements of the accused's friends. Because he was a disqualified driver his girlfriend was driving at the time and she had trouble getting the car into gear. Why hadn't the prosecutor asked this question? If only she had been able to get that car into gear it would have left the area before Craig reappeared from McDonald's and walked innocently behind the car. He didn't even kick the rear tyre which I think I would have been tempted to do. The crown prosecutor's reply to that question was, "That's irrelevant." Honestly.

A friend has told me that I must be careful not to put Craig on a pedestal. He wasn't perfect. He would leave his damp gym gear in a heap on the floor of the living room, but he was kind, considerate and generous to all who worked with him or knew him, and that hurts. Why my Craigie?

He, like all our children, was very precious. Thank goodness I had the opportunity to tell him so just three nights before he was assaulted. He had gone to the gym early in the evening as he had a client coming at 6pm. At 7pm the gym receptionist rang to ask where he was. My reply was that as we only lived 10 minutes away he must have had an accident, could she please look for him and ring me back. She did soon after, having found him in another room. Apparently she had been impressed by my concern and had said to Craig that he must be really precious. When he shared this with me on his return home that night I assured him that all our three were very precious to us both and that if anything ever happened to any of them I wouldn't be able to cope. His answer was "Don't worry about me mum, I plan to be around for a long, long time." ...If only.

Supermarket shopping is getting easier though fraught with memories of how much food Craig consumed. I am slowly getting used to only half-filling the trolley fortnightly instead of filling it weekly. I have trouble when there are young people around, particularly new graduates or school friends of Craig's, but I guess it's pretty hard for them too. Other things remain difficult too. Like certain comedies on television that Craig and I often watched together. They are no longer funny. It seems that everywhere I go I'm reminded of him.

Irreparable damage has been done to many young people through this one stupid act of violence. Craig had a wide circle of friends through university and the jobs he had. They have all been affected and the ripple effect of this tragedy is widespread.

Sometimes the pain is unbearable. I've been known to curl up into the foetal position and sob for hours at a time. I've only once considered ending it all – saved by the bell – a telephone call from a caring friend and a jolt back to reality and my responsibilities to my three surviving darlings.

I've been told by experts that time heals. I don't believe them, but I do have to admit that time does help – a little.

It's now 9.30pm and I've just finished printing the enclosed. Six hours and a box of tissues later. Sorry it's so long, there were other bits I could have included, but I did try to keep to the subject.

After serving just two years of a three year sentence, the man responsible for Craig Robertson's death was released from prison.

6

Jayne McLellan

Jayne, a 17-year-old living in Dunedin, went to a movie with a 23-year-old man known to Jayne and her brothers. After leaving the theatre Jayne was dragged into a secluded area, raped and murdered. The murder of Jayne on 17 November 1988 was a particularly brutal attack carried out over some time.

Pam Wadsworth had three children from a previous marriage, two sons and a daughter. Following that first marriage Pam had remarried and was living quietly in the Dunedin suburb of Abbotsford. On the night of 17 November 1988 Pam's life was changed forever. This is her story.

Just before 8 o'clock on that night, 23-year-old Andrew MacMillan, known to our family, rang for my 20-year-old son. He was working overtime that night and I was out visiting my mother. Jayne, my 17-year-old daughter, answered the phone.

Jayne knew MacMillan, his parents lived in the next street to us. Although we knew him I never encouraged him to come to the house. He was a bad influence on my children and I strongly suspected him of being on drugs.

MacMillan was a persistent type and asked Jayne to meet him at the nearby Green Island picture theatre. Had I been home there is no way Jayne would have been allowed out to meet him, but for some reason she decided to go. While there he gave her two "rollies" to take with an orange drink. Because there were only a few people at the theatre the management decided it wasn't warranted showing the film and it was cancelled.

Jayne and Andrew went to visit one of Jayne's friends and were on their way home in a taxi when Andrew had the driver stop at the Green Island bus depot. After getting out they walked across the road to the footbridge over the Kaikorai Stream. This was about 11pm and Jayne was never seen alive again.

There was a cut in the shoulder of Jayne's leather jacket where I believe MacMillan forced her over a fence at knife point. From there he made her walk with him under the willow trees beside the stream where he raped her, all the time cutting her on the face, neck and hands with a serrated-edged knife.

The grandmother of a 17-year-old boy who heard Jayne screaming phoned the police, but Jayne's cries for help had gone on for at least 10 minutes before the boy became concerned enough to call for help. He had walked down to a fence and while he could hear the screaming he couldn't see anything.

"Get off me, this is serious, I'm dying, call an ambulance," were the cries the boy heard and it was then he asked his grandmother to ring for the police.

I know of five witnesses who heard Jayne's cries for help and screaming which had been going on for between 10 and 20 minutes. Yet it was only the one person who phoned for help.

By the time police arrived MacMillan had just finished killing Jayne and was still standing over her partly-clothed body. She was naked from the waist down, lying face down in the water with a concrete post over the back of her head.

The police chased MacMillan up the stream and arrested him for the brutal murder of Jayne. A police officer tried to find her pulse or other signs of life but couldn't so decided to try mouth to mouth resuscitation. When he tried to open Jayne's mouth he couldn't, her jaw had been shattered. Her upper clothing had been pulled up to her neck and there were puncture marks, grazes and blood on her neck. MacMillan's clothing was wet and his face and hands were covered in Jayne's blood. When charged with her murder he had nothing to say.

My daughter died as a result of the combined effects of asphyxia from drowning and inhaling blood. This was complicated by the multiple facial injuries and a fracture to the skull. Late the next day a post-mortem was carried out on Jayne and the results make horrific reading. The report reads as follows:

On the girl's right hand were cuts which were consistent with defence wounds and an abrasion and bruising on her wrist appeared to have been caused by a bite. The girl's left nipple was almost completely separated from her breast. Examination of the wound leads me to the opinion that the injury was the result of a bite. There were extensive injuries to the girl's face and neck. While most of these injuries were superficial and not life-threatening, there would have been extensive bleeding. All these wounds to the right side of the head and neck were consistent with having been inflicted by a knife. Cuts, abrasions and bruising to the left side of the girl's head and face were the result of blunt force injury. The lower jaw had been fractured, teeth had been knocked out, and the left upper jaw was fractured and fragmented back through the hard and soft palates. The left upper jaw had been completely separated from the remaining facial bones. The left cheek bone had been fractured, as had the bone around the left eye. There were skull fractures right across the base of the skull as a result of a heavy blow with a blunt object, and there were haemorrhages in the membrane surrounding the brain and over part of the brain surface. A round smooth surface stone was located in the back of the throat, behind the main airway. It was obstructing the upper part of the gullet but there was no evidence it was obstructing the airway.

These injuries to my daughter were described as being "extreme and immediately life-threatening." They were consistent with the use of a knife and of the concrete post found behind Jayne's head. The blunt force injuries contributed to her death and even without MacMillan placing Jayne in the water she would have died anyway.

I'm not blaming anyone else for Jayne's death but I'm sure that if some of the people who had heard her screams had acted sooner she may be alive today. Please, if you ever hear screaming that sounds suspicious, phone the police for help straight away. It may save a life.

And what of us. My family is not the same any more. I have changed. I feel quite different. While my sons are now in their mid to late twenties I worry about them constantly. Both sons think about Jayne's death all the time but only one talks about it if I raise the subject, my other son never talks about it. My youngest son was even found one night, sitting beside Jayne's grave. He was the one who had to identify his sister's body and I know it's haunted him for a long time. My ex-husband and I have never spoken about Jayne's death at all.

Since that night in 1988 we've had to contend with a lot. I've lost a lot of time off work over the past four years with depression and other illnesses brought about by grief. This has caused financial difficulties which only compounded the emotional problems caused by Jayne's death. For a long time I experienced dreadful nightmares repeatedly. I could see everything, hear the screams and even feel the pain, and the desperate feelings of being unable to get Jayne away from him. I still wake up screaming but not as often as I did.

We all miss Jayne terribly. She was such a happy, bubbly personality and always playing jokes, giving hugs and kisses. She saw the best in people and was full of love, fun and caring and was a generous, helpful young lady who was popular. She mixed well with all age groups and loved animals. Jayne would have been 25 on December 6, 1995.

While we are still affected by this terrible crime it is nowhere near as bad as those first months. For instance, the day after the murder a youngish sounding man rang me and said, "Do you want to be raped before or after you are murdered?" and, "Do you want to be buried with your daughter?" Then the night before Jayne's funeral the phone rang about 11pm. It was a young girl who said, "Hello Mum, it's Jayne here, I'm not really dead, I'm coming home!" My husband overheard that conversation. I was just so shocked. Some people can be so cruel. A woman who lived just a few houses down the street told a mutual friend that she thought my daughter got what she deserved. Almost unbelievable, yet it's the same woman who's now in prison for hiring someone to kill her husband.

The coldness of MacMillan was not easy to take. He was even overheard by policemen on the morning after the murder calling out to someone in another cell at the police station. He bragged about having "boned a sheila," and "snuffed her out to stop her screaming." He referred to this 17-year-old young girl that he had raped and murdered as being a "silly bitch".

66

At his trial I wasn't called as a witness so could sit through the proceedings. Apart from a few detectives no one really knew who I was. My husband was a witness so he had to sit in a waiting room for three days. He couldn't go down the street in case he was called and during the three days wasn't even offered a cup of tea. He told me it was a cold, unfeeling atmosphere. Although he is not Jayne's natural father he treated her as his own and he misses her terribly. Jayne's murder was very, very hard on him.

In the early days I found friends walking towards me in town suddenly turn into shops or cross the road. They simply didn't know what to say to me. I can understand this but even after six years I haven't heard from some of them. At the time of Jayne's death I was working as

Jayne McLellan, murdered 17 November 1988 aged 17.

an agent for a vacuum cleaning company and was told, "Oh well Pam, you'll be able to put all this behind you now and get on with the job of selling machines!" I was also told that I was lowering the morale of the other agents. The pressure was on me to sell a certain number of machines in a month of which there were only three weeks left. No-one except the office girls wanted to understand or sympathise with what I was going through. My job was on the line and I was constantly threatened with losing it. At one stage someone from the company came to my house demanding my stock while I was out selling in the evening. The pressure was too much and I eventually handed in my notice. They just didn't seem to want anyone working for them that was caught up in a scandal of this nature. As if it were our fault! The month before Jayne died, I topped the sales in Dunedin and won myself a wall clock for my efforts. So what were they talking about?

I then got a job for four hours a day washing dishes and waiting on tables at a restaurant in Dunedin. I worked there for four months but was still suffering from shock. The management and staff knew what had happened and treated me very well. They were very understanding. What a difference! During those four months I never had one day off work except for the week of the trial. Yet every day after work I walked down Stuart Street in tears to my car. I left the restaurant because I was only getting $100 a week which wasn't enough money and the hours weren't long enough. I was working hard to pay off a debt of Jayne's, pay for part of her funeral and also a headstone for her grave. Everything was falling all around me, my car needed extensive repairs and I think I found the hardest thing was rationalising that I was saving for a headstone when I should have been saving for a daughter's wedding. I almost got my washing machine repossessed and also my car. I needed a full-time job in a hurry. Six weeks later I managed to get a job in a factory and I've been there ever since.

That began a turning point for us. A friend of mine had approached Senior Sergeant Bill O'Brien of the Dunedin police. He is heavily involved in victim support and said I had had enough contending with the grief and shock of Jayne's horrible death. Through his efforts, negotiations with Social Welfare and the ACC and contacts he had in the community, the headstone was paid for. The monumental mason, Mr Ian Bingham, sent a photo of Jayne to Italy to have a ceramic picture done for the headstone. He donated this free of charge and I found it a lovely gesture and appreciated it very much.

I started to realise there were some nice people out there and at last the weight began to lift from my shoulders. Earlier on I had been to the ACC myself and was told there was nothing for me, but if Jayne had lived, then she would have received a cheque once a month and so would I because I would have had to have taken care of her. I have been desperate in all sorts of ways. I went to Social Welfare to see if there was any help available but no, nothing. Except the whole murder thing was a fascination to the woman behind the desk when she asked if I had a photo of my daughter which I showed her. She then called out to one of her office friends about the photo being of the girl who was murdered at Green Island. I just wasn't myself at all and didn't have the strength to say anything about feeling humiliated. I then turned to walk out and was absolutely shocked when I saw the long queue of people behind me waiting to be served. They must have heard

68

everything that this woman was saying because she spoke so loudly.

Since Jayne's death I hear the same old comments. "To put all this behind you, and get on with your life." "Now that you are over your daughter's death how do you feel when you see a murderer's face on TV?" "Oh well, life's like that isn't it?" A friend even says quite often, "You have the best public face I've ever seen."

I'm now making an effort to get on with my life and keep my family happy. I've been working for Cadbury's since the 12th of June 1989 and the management and staff are friendly and really great. Despite getting on with life it can't take away the memories of losing Jayne in such a terrible way. Perhaps the following notice in the memorial column of the newspaper sums up how I feel:

IN MEMORY OF JAYNE
May tender memories soften our grief,
May fond recollections bring us relief,
And may we find comfort and peace
In the thought of the joy
That knowing our precious Jayne brought –
For time and space can never divide,
Or keep our loved ones from our side.
When memory paints in colours true,
The happy hours we had with you.

And what of Andrew MacMillan. He was described as having an abnormal personality. His life sentence will probably end around 1998. Personally I hope he never comes out, not just because of Jayne's death but because he could do it again. I've been told he has a temper and just won't take no for an answer. I often wonder if he would know or even care what effect he has had on our family. The actions of that man took the life of an innocent 17-year-old girl. When you lose a daughter to an illness or accident it's very hard. To know your daughter died in such a violent way seems even harder. I hope that what I've said here helps people understand what the family of a murder victim goes through.

In October 1993, less than five years after Andrew MacMillan killed Jayne he was seen by neighbours visiting his mother in Abbotsford. MacMillan had been transferred from Christchurch Prison to Dunedin so he could have visiting rights to his sick mother. He was seen in the garden of her home talking to her as she tended the plants. Two prison officers sat in a van across the road watching from a distance. Pam Wadsworth was angry and frightened. Angry that this man she regards as a monster can be out on visits so soon after such a brutal murder and frightened at what she feels is a lack of security. Had Mrs MacMillan been gravely ill such visits might be seen as humane and for her sake. But Pam Wadsworth knows that is not the case and knowing this murderer is being driven around so close to where she works gives her a very uneasy feeling. (Through continuing illness brought on by grief at losing her daughter in such a traumatic way, Pam has now had to leave her place of employment).

7

Daniel Fleming

Hokio beach near Levin was the scene of a New Year family gathering in 1992. Daniel Fleming disturbed someone stealing food from the property and was fatally stabbed. Occurring just after midnight, Daniel's death was the first of a rash of murders in the early months of 1992.

Hi, my name is Vicky and I'm writing this to tell people what happened to my husband Danny on the morning of 1 January, 1992 in Hokio, near Levin, and the effect it had on me and my life.

It was New Year's Eve 1991. It is a sort of tradition in Danny's family, every New Year's Eve we all go to Hokio where Danny's grandparents own a beach property. There we would spend New Year together. That year was no different and I can remember a lot of things about the afternoon and evening. Danny finished work around 5pm and he came home and rang Hokio just to see what the weather was like. It was raining in Paraparaumu so he wanted to make sure it wasn't raining in Levin. We were told that the weather was great so we loaded up our dog Star, and Danny's trail bike and left Paraparaumu at 7pm. We had borrowed the firm's truck (even though we shouldn't have been using it) so we could take the trail bike.

We arrived at Hokio about 7.30pm. Most people were already there by then, basically close family and friends. A little later on Danny

71

came over to me and asked if he could take the trail bike for a ride down the beach. I can remember thinking at the time, why is he asking me if he can go for a ride? It certainly wasn't like him. He took Star and went for a ride and arrived back half an hour later with a surfboard stuck under his bum on the back of the bike. He had seen it lying on the beach and thought Cindy and Tracy (his nieces) would like it. The night progressed on and everyone seemed to be having a good time. That year there seemed to be more family than friends at Hokio. In previous years I'd always felt a little bit left out, mainly because everyone had been going there almost since they were born. This was the first year that I really enjoyed myself. Danny was looking after me most of the night, bringing me drinks and making sure I was okay. I can also remember the way Star stayed so close to Danny all night, he just followed him around everywhere and watched him the whole night.

We all saw the New Year in, including Danny's grandparents who left soon after midnight. About 1am Danny and I went to bed. But from there on things get a little hazy. I can remember Danny getting out of bed to get me a drink of water, and then I must have fallen asleep. The next thing I remember is someone waking me up and taking me up the driveway to the road. There seemed to people everywhere and Danny was just lying on the road not moving. I remember kneeling on the road and taking his hand and talking to him. I kept expecting him to sit up and answer me, or squeeze my hand to let me know everything was going to be all right. I tried talking to him about Star and all the things we had planned to do, like having kids and going overseas together. When he didn't move or answer me I can remember thinking I've got to get him angry. If he's angry he'll fight back so I tried yelling at him.

Then someone put me in the ambulance with Danny and I held his hand and talked to him all the way back to Levin. I don't know where they took us but they took Danny away and I was in a room and they were asking me to sign a piece of paper identifying Danny. All I wanted to do was be with him. At first they wouldn't let me but finally they let me see him again and I'll never forget that. He was lying on a sort of table with a white sheet over him. For the first time I saw the blood and can remember looking at his feet and seeing blood all over them. That's when it really hit me that he was dead and he wasn't going to sit up and say it was all just a joke.

The next thing I recall is sitting in the police station trying to remember someone's phone number to get hold of Mum and Dad. I remember thinking I only want Danny, if he was here everything would be all right. But Mum and Dad were staying in the Marlborough Sounds on a launch, they had a cellphone but I couldn't remember the number. The only number I could remember was my Auntie Trisha's in Palmerston North. By this time it must have been 5.30 or 6am and I'm not sure what I said to Auntie Trisha but she and my cousin came out to Hokio almost straight away. The police took us back to Hokio and I stayed there until my parents arrived in the afternoon. Someone had managed to get hold of them and they flew up immediately. I just felt so lost

Daniel Fleming and his wife Vicky just eight months before his death.

and didn't know what I wanted to do or where I wanted to go and that feeling stayed with me for a long time. I felt like a part of me was missing.

The rest of that week is a blur. I got through the funeral and everyone coming around to see me and in some ways that was the hardest thing to deal with. I just felt like shutting myself away from everyone and I was sick and tired of being polite. I know I've been quite lucky to have my family around me, some people are not so lucky. One thing this tragedy has done is to bring me much closer to Danny's family.

About two weeks after Danny was murdered, I went back to our house. It was hard going home but I didn't really feel at home at my parents' place. I was lucky to have Star with me, he's been good company ever since Danny died. At times he can be a responsibility that I don't really want, but most of the time I'm glad to have him there. The first few weeks back at home I kept expecting Danny to walk in the door. Every night when I got home from work, I would expect to see his truck parked outside and all the lights on in the house like it used to be. It took a lot of adjusting coming home to an empty house. I'm not sure when I finally accepted that Danny was gone and that he wasn't coming back. In some ways I think it was after the trial was over and the murderer had been convicted.

Danny being murdered has changed me and my life in a lot of ways. We had been together for four years when he was murdered, and had been married for only nine months. We had built our own house the year before and everything seemed to be going really well. We were planning on having a family in a year or so and these were the things that kept going through my mind. All our plans were gone. Most of the time I just felt like giving it all up and killing myself too. I didn't want to be here if I couldn't be with Danny and I used to think that if things had happened the other way around he would have been able to cope much better. I know now that's not true, he would just have coped in another way.

In some ways the only thing that's kept me going is having Star and our house. I kept thinking how much Star had meant to Danny and therefore it was my responsibility to look after him. In a lot of ways this has made me stronger. I have had to learn to be by myself again and to cope with things that I would have just let Danny do. I have had to push myself to do certain things and people always used to say to me, "It gets easier with time," and I always thought they didn't know what they were talking about. How could it possibly get easier, but gradually it has. I never forget, it's just the times between crying get longer. Some days even now I still miss him so much, but in a different way to how it was in the beginning. I miss his friendship and support, and just being able to talk to him and to have him talk back to me.

For the first year I always felt that Danny was around and he was looking out for me. It has only been the last few months that I have felt he is not so close. I think that is because I am finally starting to let go of him and learning to get on with my own life now. For the first time I am starting to feel that I am ready to get on with my life and I know deep down that's what Danny would want for me. I have learnt from all this that life is just too short to spend my time doing something I'm not happy doing, I have to make the most of the opportunities that present themselves. I have noticed one thing that has changed about me, I no longer feel able to plan things too far

74

ahead. I feel in some ways that is tempting fate if I plan too much and that it won't happen. I have also found it very difficult to get close to new people. I don't want to put myself in a position to get hurt again and I'm slowly learning to relax but it's something I think I will always be a little wary of. I don't want to become too dependent on another person again.

Daniel Fleming's death was so unnecessary. What actually happened was that during the New Year's Eve celebrations a group of young people known to one of the extended family arrived and asked to stay. They were made welcome but unknown to everyone at the barbecue, within their midst was a killer who was to strike later that night. Danny's mother recalled events of that first day of 1992 so well.

Danny and Star.

Danny was a fine man, 6 foot 2 inches tall and strongly built. Earlier that year he had married a beautiful young woman called Vicky and they lived together in a house they built in Paraparaumu. They both worked hard on the home, garden and landscaping. In his garage was a home gym where Danny kept fit for his softball and swimming.

As usual Christmas was spent as a family where we made a home video and planned to meet at Hokio for the New Year's Eve get-together. Apart from nine years when Danny went to Brisbane he never missed our family New Year celebrations. For 30 years he had made that annual pilgrimage to Hokio. I saw my son on the beach on the afternoon of 31 December, his dog Star on the motorbike. He was so happy. Friends and family gathered and at one stage there were about 40 of us having a barbecue and sing-a-long. The night was warm and the children played. After the younger ones went to bed around 9.30pm a group turned up and joined us. Had we known that a potential, knife carrying murderer was amongst them we would not have made them welcome.

At midnight Danny kissed me for the last time and said, "I love you Mum." Not long after that he kissed his grandparents goodnight. "Drive carefully," he called out to them as they left. Only a few people remained around the barbecue, most had gone to bed, including Danny and Vicky.

Soon after 3am Danny's uncle called out to him, "Someone's stealing from your ute." Danny leapt out of bed and ran out to the caravan to confront the thief. The next moment my son-in-law was calling out that Danny had been stabbed. When we ran out to the road I saw my son lying on the cold, hard surface. Vicky was holding his hand as others began crying and calling out. I looked down at my beautiful son, so strong and tall, lying on this hard road. This was no way to die. My daughter was crying and my younger son just stood by so quiet and white looking. It tore me apart to see my children and the pain in their eyes. When Danny was placed in the ambulance I asked the doctor, "Is my son dead?"

"Yes he is," was the reply. I felt so sick looking at my son's body which was now turning blue and hearing the cries of "no Danny no," coming from his lovely wife.

What an incredible waste. To kill a man over a chilly bin of food. Who would do such a thing – what kind of person could do it? After we had offered them hospitality they stole from us and when confronted the killer took a knife and fatally stabbed my son.

We spent the next several hours at the Levin police station and while the police were excellent to us we couldn't get hold of my youngest son. He had gone tramping in North Auckland and I couldn't let him find out about his brother's death on the news. But the details of Danny's murder appeared in the news that night, even his name. The television showed the bloodstained road where Danny's life had seeped away. My youngest son was listening to the news in Whangarei at 9.30 the next morning when he learned of his big brother's murder. What a hellish way to find out such devastating news.

The young man who murdered my son had been arrested before for carrying a knife. Police even said to us that they had told the Justice Department he would kill someone one day – and he did. He stabbed

Danny three times by plunging the knife first in his back, then in the groin and finally through Danny's heart. What kind of person can do that? What kind of person laughs when he's found guilty and gets life imprisonment?

Four hundred people came to my son's funeral and we finally placed his ashes to rest on what would have been his first wedding anniversary. To my mind there is still an injustice. We are hurting and it will go on for the rest of our lives. No longer can my son ring me or come home on Mother's Day. New years at Hokio will never be the same happy family affairs again.

And the person who did this to us? We all know what 'life' means and it doesn't mean life. But we also know what death means and it's final.

Just six months before Daniel Fleming died, his killer had appeared in court for sentencing having been found guilty of wounding with intent to cause grievous bodily harm. On that occasion he had stabbed a man with a knife.

8

The Ratima Tragedy

Masterton, Friday 26 June, 1992. Raymond Ratima, in a fit of jealousy, killed his wife's brother, pregnant sister, her de facto husband and infant son. He then turned his attention to his own three sons, killing in all seven people. He then lay in wait for his wife and her parents and all but succeeded in killing them. After pleading guilty he received life imprisonment.

In cases of murder there is almost always a 'ripple' effect where repercussions of the crime affects a wide range of people. Often those most closely involved receive the attention and support. As the ripple effect widens so the support lessens. This chapter features Debbie Woodward, the sister-in-law of Raymond Ratima. Her parents and only surviving sister, Ratima's wife, were naturally the focus of attention having lost their children in the dreadful events of that Friday night. But for Debbie much of the responsibility for sorting out the aftermath of this tragedy fell on her shoulders. Her story describes the ripple effect succinctly...

Grief is such an unimaginable trauma yet each and everyone of us will at some time in our lives be faced with it. As if the loss of a loved one was not enough to contend with, families of murder victims face the rigours of an investigation and the prosecution process. Upon sentence of life imprisonment one should find solace in the fact that the offender will be out of the way forever, but this is a bittersweet pill we have to swallow as we all know life means little more than 10 years.

A life sentence will always be the subject of continual debate but there are crimes so horrendous that life has to be just that. The introduction of degrees of murder would be a starting point for a fairer justice system especially in cases of murder as grave as that which was thrust upon our family by my brother-in-law, Raymond Ratima.

We were to have been in Masterton on the night Raymond killed most of my family. We were living in Waiouru at the time and for some reason my husband said we were not going. I wasn't happy about it but accepted his decision. Who knows what would have happened had we been there?

After we were contacted about the terrible tragedy that night we drove down to Masterton and I kept thinking it can't have happened, that it must be a bad dream. I just couldn't comprehend the magnitude of what happened. But then it came over the radio and I knew it had to be real. It's strange what thoughts you have at a time like this but I remember thinking about how could we pay for seven funerals. Yet I didn't feel any one emotion as I had no physical evidence all these people were dead. It was just so hard to comprehend.

I thought Dad would cope, he's a rock, but when I saw Dad he just broke down completely and kept going on about my brother who had been killed. If that was how Dad was reacting, who was going to look after us? I just had to put my emotions on hold. My brother and sister were dead, my other sister Toni had lost her three children and she, along with Mum and Dad, had been Raymond's next intended victims. I was the oldest of the children and much was left up to me.

The police had to interview Dad and even 12 hours after the event no one knew exactly what had happened. I was given a brief outline of what had taken place and from there on had to take things as they came. Organising seven funerals and looking after my sister and parents' welfare took its toll. They were in no shape to do anything and I had to get a doctor to visit them at the marae.

A meeting was held at the marae when the undertaker got up to speak about the need for postmortems to be carried out. Some people were pretty upset about the sensitivity issues and how the bodies had to be on the marae at a certain time. I remember standing up and saying, as far as I was concerned we had a court case to face up to and no one was going to rush the pathologist. One slip up from him by being rushed could see Raymond walk free on a technicality and I wasn't prepared to take the risk.

While a lot of people didn't like it, I said are you going to be there for us after the funerals are over? As it turned out, none of them were.

Dad said I was to make all the decisions for our family and at the time I didn't care whose toes I stood on. As far as I was concerned there were a lot of people there who couldn't give a damn about the kids while they were alive so they were not going to have a say now they were dead. A lot of friction was generated on the marae due to the media being camped outside. If anyone spoke to the media it had to be as they saw it and not as representatives of the family.

I felt our family got a lot of flak from the public, not that it was entirely their fault. They were simply making judgements on the facts they had been given. That was a hard thing to deal with, the media. But the police helped a lot by having media liaison people assisting us.

Viewing the bodies was a terribly difficult experience. I didn't know what to expect except knowing they had all died horrifically. Toni insisted on seeing her three sons and although I tried to convince her to remember them as they were, she insisted. I wanted just my parents and sister to view the family and share a private moment of grief. But there were a lot of people at the viewing. It was too much for Mum, Dad and Toni and they stayed at the marae. As if seeing all seven dead wasn't enough the thing that upset me was seeing my younger brother. He had died first and had put up a struggle against Raymond. When I looked around I could see what it was he had put up such a struggle for. He died for the rest of us and there he was, all alone. People were sitting with all the other bodies but no one was with him. It wasn't fair so I sat with him but felt I couldn't say goodbye to my sister or nephews. Everybody else was with them and I felt I didn't want to invade their grief. It was a very difficult time.

I had been put into the position of making decisions. Being a Maori funeral I had elders coming up to me telling me I couldn't cry; I had to be strong for Mum and Dad. So I'd sit at the back of the marae crying as I was tired of people telling me to shut up. I thought to myself, that was my brother and sister in there ... and all of my nephews. Over half our family wiped out and I was supposed to feel nothing. Other thoughts invaded me. Like believing that as the eldest

I should have been there protecting them but in reality knowing if I had been there I would have died too. I believe that if Raymond hadn't done it that night he would have done it some time later.

Things were compounded further. My husband stood by me but later, when I couldn't suppress my emotions any more, the pressure came on and we temporarily separated. Thankfully that didn't last for long and we came together again.

I know Toni lost her children but my brother, sister and nephews also died. So much of the focus goes on to Toni and many people have done so much to help her and my parents. What disappoints me is that they haven't done enough to help themselves. So far they've done nothing positive to change the way they live and when you go through events like we all did, I believe you have to come to grips with it. I know blame should not be placed anywhere. Raymond was a member of our family which makes it different were he a person we didn't know.

Although there were factors that led to Raymond killing our family it was ultimately his choice on the night. He has to take responsibility for the choices he made but I just feel we could now live our lives differently. I also believe as a society we have to prevent this sort of thing happening again. Domestic violence plays too much part in people's lives and in society. If people don't learn to come to grips with this then the kind of tragedy we are involved in can happen again.

If only my family would take advantage of counselling offered to them rather than trying to deal with this in other ways. They have to understand that it wasn't their fault and that Raymond is basically a weak person who resorted to violence to solve his conflicts. What he did really epitomises family violence and he took it to the extreme, lashing out at innocent people. My parents and Toni have to see it that way. That they were not responsible.

I believe there is a light at the end of the tunnel and you can lead a full life eventually. But you have to help yourself get through the tunnel first. While I haven't reached that point yet I'm optimistic. I don't want to be a victim but rather a survivor. As far as I'm concerned the victims are dead. I don't believe the pain ever goes but you do learn to live with it and to put it in its place.

I've got personal thoughts on aspects of ACC. I don't want to challenge them over issues such as counselling, for if I did I would then regard myself as a victim and in a way Raymond will have beaten me. While I won't let that happen I do feel there are inconsistencies in the ACC rules that affect me and others whose families have been involved in murder. Not only did I have the losses to contend with and the grief associated with it, I also had to shoulder the responsibility of dealing with the aftermath, making decisions for the family, arranging seven funerals and other tasks. I accept that I had to do those things but for the only other survivors of the night, Toni and my parents, they got access to counselling. Yet I've had to pay for my own. With three young children that has not been easy.

Of course the buck of helping has to stop somewhere but in cases of murder it is not just the immediate family. They have to speak to someone, usually a close relative, who then has to shoulder some pretty heavy emotions. And I am not just talking about our case, it happens in many families facing the aftermath of dealing with murder. Close relatives such as grandparents hurt every bit as much. I do not feel government policy caters for those people who are perhaps one step removed. People don't know how to deal with emotional pain automatically. If we did we wouldn't need counsellors. It's just not part of our make-up.

I am not asking for compensation. I do not expect a dollar value to be put on the loss of my family. I do want someone to realise that people like me need financial support. At $120 an hour how can you say I will put money aside for counselling? Emotions are not like a tap you turn on and off. When a moment of grief hits you, you have to go with it and not say no, I can't afford it this week. It doesn't work like that.

If you push your emotions away it causes more problems. To get ACC help I would have to do something to myself or my children. How bizarre, having to start the cycle off again just to get help. As it turned out I organised things for myself. I gave up fighting the ACC rather than have to recount my story of what happened to people who probably don't really care and are seen as sitting in judgement of me. I'm not on trial. The person who did all this has been sentenced, so why am I made to feel like I'm on trial, to justify the pain I am feeling. I know that others in similar situations have those same feelings of being judged and it is not fair. I think the 'system' has to acknowledge this and work around it.

Everyone's emotions are different and cannot be generalised. Because some people are one or two steps removed from the murder victim it does not follow that these people necessarily feel any less pain than those more closely related. Personally I feel very together and very sane but sometimes get the impression people think you have to be mad to want help. Throughout this ordeal my husband and in-laws have helped the most and they know all of those who died. As an example my in-laws took my children for a week, keeping them away from the media. My boys are of a similar age to their cousins who died and at times I feel guilty when I have them around Toni. But then I cannot be made to feel guilt because of what Raymond did.

We are left behind to deal with his consequences. Yet I actually forgive Raymond for what he did. Hate is too strong an emotion for me. One day I rang the prison as we heard Raymond had got a bashing from other prisoners. I just wanted to make sure he was all right, yet the person I spoke to accused me of being vengeful. Vengeful over the telephone? All I did was ring up out of concern for his welfare. I have heard that he is all right and if he's having a bad time he only has to ask to be locked up. I have also been told that when the going gets tough he can ask for help and someone comes in to counsel him. I thought to myself, "Oh, good for him – I'm glad some of my taxes are going to helping him because they are sure not helping me!" I know he is incarcerated and that's got to be hard but he gets three meals a day and a roof over his head which is more than he had on the outside. If he needs psychiatric help it's there for him. On the other hand if I need it I have to budget or justify to someone else that I need help. It's back to front isn't it? My husband had been told the full extent of the killings and luckily as he was with the army he was able to get counselling. He couldn't share the facts of the killings with me as at the time I didn't want to know. While he received counselling I was able to speak to a social worker at the camp. Other than that I have paid for any counselling needs myself.

And what of Raymond? The possibility of him getting parole in a few years is frightening. It is the first time in my life I have lived with fear. To look at Raymond he's nothing. Although he was building himself up he was still a small man. But I've seen the result of his anger and what someone can do. It's frightening. I couldn't stop him even if I tried. I know 'they' talk of rehabilitation but not in this case. I just don't believe it. Of course when he is released he will have parole conditions, but that is small comfort to me. He only has to break them and if he is determined he could do so easily.

Emotions can be mixed. When I saw Raymond on television after his arrest he was kissing the air defiantly and I thought that's not Raymond. Then I saw him at sentencing and that was the real

Raymond. I know the day he was sentenced for seven killings that one day he would be released. And I also believe that in an ideal world he should be locked up forever. Why should he get a second chance? Those he killed never got a chance, they are dead and gone and won't ever be coming back.

Our views will be sought every year he is due for parole and that means having to relive what happened every 12 months. I want to get to a point where I have dealt with all the emotions, retain memories of my family and live a full life without going through the process each year. How can people involved in cases of murder really deal with the issues when the murderer is still around? One of my biggest fears in saying what I have said is how people will judge me. The same old story, what would she know? She didn't lose her kids. I'm tired of being judged and I felt I was judged even by my family when the others died. Others are full of hate and think I am crazy forgiving Raymond, but it does not mean to say I condone what he did. I do not condone his actions but if you live with hate it is like a cancer. I forgive him but don't forget what he has done and what he has taken away. And I do not say forgive him and let him out, no way! As families of murder victims we have numerous 'battles' to fight. The final so-called battle is the fight with inner peace. To come to terms with death due to violence is one of the hardest 'battles' one would face in a lifetime. You never get over what has happened but you learn to live with it. Grief can bring people together in an appreciation of life and love or it can destroy a family leaving only a shell of a once happy, loving family. When I write down my experiences now I find they are becoming more brief. I realise how tiring the 'battles' can be. The emotional drain is immense.

I want people to read this, not to be judgemental but to say this is wrong, this is unfair. Because it is.

A sister of my mother wrote the following poem after the loss of our family. It has given me comfort at times and perhaps it will also give comfort to others who have lost loved ones as they go through the inevitable hard times.

THE TREE
The tree that once stood proud and tall
Now surrenders to the breeze
Which gently blows in and through its leaves
Wherever it will please.

The tree is big and broad but now
There is a gap left there
Right down below where young shoots grow
And buds don't yet appear.

The wound that's left now openly weeps
For the branch that now has gone
And the tree is limp from the sudden shock
Of a scar it now must don.

Mr Gardener, would you please come
And heal this wound of mine
Says the tree to God who hears all prayers
And whose healing is divine.

God gently takes the branch in hand
And with loving tender care
Breathes life again into the tree
Whose pain it cannot bear.

Please know dear tree, that this thy grief
Was not of my own hand
But of one, whose deeds are known
In this and other lands.

But I am come that you may know
That joy and peace can be
Restored to you by my great love
Both true and abundantly.

Look up dear tree and know that soon
You will stand tall again
For the peace and gladness that I give
Shall evermore remain.

As for the branch that once was yours
It's here now at my side
So beautiful and radiant
It shall evermore reside.

                    Elizabeth Reiri-Rongonui

I would like to take this opportunity to acknowledge those who are rarely thought of, yet affected by this tragedy, and also their families who have helped them through their personal trauma. To Luther Toloa, the police officer in charge of the enquiry, the detectives, other police officers and judicial officers who were involved with this case. Also Dr Matt Mills, the attending physician on the night of the tragedy. To David Lindsay for his support and advice and to all the cousins, aunts, uncles, grandparents and friends of the victims.

To all the members of the Ferguson, Reiri, Harmon and Nia Nia families who have helped me to deal with my loss while having to cope themselves.

Finally special thanks to my husband Paul, my own children and the Woodward family who have taught me there is love and life after a tragedy. Thanks Ma and Pa.

9

Eric Lowe

When Eric Lowe remonstrated with his daughter's former boyfriend the result was Mr Lowe's death and a life sentence for the boyfriend. On 18 January 1992, Mr Lowe was knocked over by a car which then ran him over causing fatal injuries.

One might expect that when someone is convicted of murder and sentenced to life imprisonment they would be unable to contact the victim's family. But that is far from so and the case involving Eric Lowe's death illustrates how easy it is for contact to be made.

The offender in this case was a 29-year-old man who had had a relationship with Brenda Lowe, daughter of Eric. The couple had a daughter and sometime after she was born the relationship cooled considerably.

On the night of 18 January, Brenda, her daughter, father and other friends were driving on a Taranaki road when the offender's car appeared. Earlier in the day there had been numerous acrimonious phone calls between the offender and Brenda Lowe where he issued threats until eventually Mr Lowe told him not to ring again. According to a witness the offender drove his car at the Lowe vehicle in a frightening manner, subsequently colliding with them. Mr Lowe got out of the car he was in and had to step out of the way as the offender's car reversed at him. The car was then driven straight at Mr

Lowe, knocking him to the ground. The driver then accelerated over him, rolling him under the car, before disappearing around a corner. Mr Lowe died of head injuries as a result of being run over.

Following the court case the offender was found guilty of murder and sentenced to imprisonment for life. Since then Brenda Lowe has had to contend with even more than the loss of her father and the fact she witnessed the murder...

I am constantly living in fear that he will get out and I don't think my fear is misplaced. I have good reason to be worried. He had often told me he would do away with me. He also said he would throw our daughter 'off the bridge'. I believe that I was meant to be the one he wanted to kill. I live on my own with two children and so far he's contacted me by phone and in writing. The first letter I got was really quite destructive and was addressed to my little girl. As if it wasn't bad enough that she had to be there when her father ran over her grandfather. Now she gets mail from him.

He also has access to a telephone and was calling me but I just want to be left alone. Some people might think that I am over-reacting but if they saw the sorts of things in his letters they might understand.

But of the things that worry me the most it is his being kept in New Plymouth Prison. Early in 1994 there were three escapes in a very short time and I've objected to his being kept here but without success. A letter from the Minister of Justice said that my ex-boyfriend is classified as a 'low medium' security risk but this is not much comfort to me. The minister also said in his letter:

> "It is considered that a managed programme of reintegration, by way of 'privileges' attached to security rating, poses less risk to the community than a sudden release from imprisonment, without such a graduated approach. Thus inmates can be monitored on their response to various 'privileges', such as the freedom to associate with other inmates, their participation in various programmes and to work within the institution unsupervised. This programme is aimed at reducing the risk of reoffending.
>
> New Plymouth Prison is a regional prison, and, where possible, inmates with family in the area are retained, in order that family contact and support is maintained. This family component is seen as an important component of the

Eric Lowe (inset) and family (from left to right), Daughter Brenda, son Tony, wife Jean and daughters Suzanne and Mary. Courtesy the Daily News

rehabilitative process, and is encouraged, providing security is not compromised.

In the case of the particular inmate you refer to, his institutional behaviour does not at present give cause for concern, and he would appear to be appropriately placed for security purposes. Security classifications and appropriate placements are regularly reviewed by the institution ..."

Again, the emphasis is on his needs and not ours. From the tone of the Minister's letter it seems that we haven't got anything to worry about or to fear. Well I believe we have. Only weeks before he wrote that letter there was an article in the *Daily News*. That article was about recent escapes from New Plymouth Prison which is rated low medium to minimum for security. The manager of the prison was reported as saying that he couldn't say whether or not the remaining 98 prisoners, 12 of whom were on remand, were a potential danger to the public. He is quoted as saying, 'Some of them may be, particularly those on remand.' He also is quoted as having said, 'It was not surprising there were holes in New Plymouth Prison's security. It is the oldest operational prison in New Zealand. Modern systems are having to cope with old configurations.' The prison is 107 years old and the manager himself says there are holes in the security. I think I've got every reason to feel worried. The prison authorities might think my ex-boyfriend is a low medium risk and that his institutional behaviour doesn't give cause for concern, but then they never saw him kill my father, did they?

During 1994 Telecom moved to prevent inmates ringing people without their knowledge or running up bills. They were to install card operated telephones in prisons that would ensure inmates complied with telephone use rules. Tighter controls were needed to stop crime, intimidation of the public and the huge bills for inmates' families because of collect calls and reverse charges. Under the new system inmates would be able to dial only from an approved list of telephone numbers and out-going calls could only be made with a pre-paid Telecom phone card and the duration of the calls would be restricted. When recipients got the phone call they would be alerted by a pre-recorded message saying the call is coming from an inmate and they will be able to decline the call. At any time a recipient will be able to ask to have their name and number removed from the system. The system would also be providing a printout so prison staff can monitor the use of telephones by inmates. In May 1995 this system came into effect in one Auckland prison and if found suitable will be made available in other prisons.

10

Lindsay Gooch

During an argument in a Dunedin street on 4 April, 1992, Lindsay Gooch was punched unconscious and kicked in the head while lying on the ground. He died of the injuries and two youths were charged with manslaughter.

There are occasions when miscarriages of justice seem to occur and where the circumstances are at odds with the judicial system. One such case occurred in a Dunedin street in the early hours of an April morning.

Lindsay Gooch died from what was clearly a serious attack, yet because of the law two men charged with manslaughter walked free.

Many of the witnesses to that "incident" were intoxicated and their stories were conflicting, but a friend of the deceased was clear as to what happened. In brief the two men were in a car when they were abused by some young people. After stopping at traffic lights the younger men were seen running up to the vehicle in what was described as a threatening manner. The witness and Lindsay Gooch got out of the car believing they would be attacked in it. Both men were then set upon with punches and kicks.

"Then there was a hell of a bang, like Lindsay had been hit really hard," his friend had said in evidence. On falling to the ground Lindsay was kicked in the head.

Lindsay Gooch.

One of the questions of law was who killed Lindsay Gooch. Was it the punch? Was his death caused by hitting his head on the footpath or had a kick to the head caused him to die?

Despite defence claims of self-defence or who hit who, it is clear that Lindsay Gooch's life ended after being hit and kicked. This turned out to be a difficult case to prosecute but it certainly did nothing to satisfy Lindsay's sister's need for justice.

Wendy McDonald believed then and still does that someone should have been held responsible for her brother's death. She also believes strongly that we can never come to grips in society when our streets are unsafe as was evident in Dunedin that April morning. She has trouble rationalising with the law that saw the accused walk free.

Perhaps the main area of contention for her is the fact that the pathologist could not determine whether the punch or the kick caused the fatal injury.

"We were stunned when the judge said you couldn't convict the person who did the kicking if the punch caused the death. Likewise you couldn't convict the puncher if it was the kick that caused the fatal blow," she said. Wendy wrote to the crown prosecutor for an explanation. The fact that an altercation took place was not in dispute but because various witnesses to the incident had consumed alcohol and many gave conflicting accounts, it became difficult to establish just what had happened. In his reply to Wendy's letter the crown prosecutor said:

At the completion of the evidence there were clearly differing accounts as to what exactly had occurred. It did appear however that the most probable sequence was that the first accused struck your brother knocking him to the ground apparently causing him to lose consciousness and then the second accused subsequently joined the incident and may well have kicked him in the head. In these circumstances His Honour the Judge ruled that neither accused could be a party to the other's assault and that in essence because the pathologist could not determine which blow was the cause of death His Honour would direct the jury that neither accused could be convicted of manslaughter on the basis of separate and independent assaults. You will appreciate that the Crown must accept His Honour's rulings at trial and once this direction was given to the jury it became very difficult, if not impossible, for them to have returned a verdict of guilty...

Under our system of law a person is entitled to be acquitted unless the Crown can prove beyond any reasonable doubt that the person is guilty. This is a very high standard of proof and a jury's decision to acquit does not mean or should not be taken as a finding that the two accused did not either commit some act towards your brother or that he was effectively responsible for his own death. Rather it means that the Crown was not able to satisfy the jury to the very high standard that the law requires that the two accused were guilty.

While that is the legal position it did nothing to help Wendy McDonald. To her the system has failed her. She looks at things from a practical viewpoint not a legal one and she is far from satisfied. She says...

Lindsay was a very talented man who loved music, playing in Dunedin bands since he was at school. He was an insurance agent in his late thirties. Lindsay was an above average athlete and rugby player. He was so popular, about 700 people attended his funeral.

During the court case we had to sit with the offender's family and it was terrible. All the time we were made to feel that we had done something to them, that it was our fault their relative was up on a charge. We had to sit and watch them smirking and laughing.

During the depositions we had to ask to attend because one of those charged was only 16 at the time and the Youth Court was used. It was only when we got to the main trial that the High Court was used.

To the lay person it seems ridiculous for a judge to ask a jury to compare the size of the deceased against the accused. They were both streetwise, not little boys. They killed my brother for Heaven's sake. Another thing that upset me and seemed so ridiculous was how case law from last century can be used to compare a case in the 1990s.

We weren't happy with the prosecution yet we had no choice. Not like the accused who could choose the defence they wanted. Everything is done for the accused, right from the start. We really feel the justice system has failed us and don't believe Lindsay got a fair deal at all. Another thing that sickened me was how a month after the case one of the accused was in court on 13 charges including assaulting a policewoman. He appeared as a first offender yet a month earlier we had been in court hearing evidence of how he had killed my brother. It's just not fair.

Following the death of her brother and the court case, Wendy McDonald joined in to gather signatures for the petition. She said people virtually fell over each other trying to sign it. To her it was a sign that New Zealanders had had enough of our violent society. Later on she spoke at Parliament when the petition was presented.

The theme of her speech was simple. New Zealand is not a safe place. There is too much violence and the rights of the accused, to her mind, still prevail over the victims far too heavily.

It is a dreadful irony that Lindsay Gooch, who had been so good with other people's children, should die at a time when it was his turn to enjoy his own. When he died Lindsay left a five-year-old stepdaughter, a two-year-old son and a baby daughter of only six weeks. To his sister Wendy it seems so unfair that her brother was denied the opportunity to watch his children grow and to share in their lives as it was for them to be denied a wonderful father.

11

Anthony Thomas

A few weeks before Christmas 1989, Tony Thomas was stabbed twice in the heart with what was believed to be a sharpened screwdriver. The attack which killed Tony saw three gang members appear in court on murder charges. On conviction for manslaughter the longest sentence any of the three got was less than four years.

On a quiet Saturday morning Joy Thomas was interrupted as she mowed the lawns. It was the police with news of her son Tony. At 19 years of age Tony had had his ups and downs. Following a breakup with his girlfriend he had returned home to live, but on the Friday evening went on his usual outing to town.

The following day was to be his last session at the periodic detention centre after which he planned to go with a friend to the South Island. They were to go fruit picking, staying in a mobile home as they travelled around. Tony never came home from his Friday night in town.

So it was a shock when the police told Joy a body had been found and they thought it was her son Tony. Although they were sure, formal identification had to be made and it wasn't until the Sunday that it was shown beyond doubt that the body found was Tony Thomas.

"I really don't remember much about those first few days," said

Joy Thomas. "I do remember arranging to have Tony's body home for a few days before the funeral and was shocked at the cuts and bruises on him."

The funeral was difficult for the family. Joy travelled in the hearse with her dead son and she noticed TV cameras and reporters. Suddenly she felt invaded and although they kept their distance she was uncomfortable. From the time police told her of her son's murder until the funeral, Joy had not eaten and, apart from being distraught, she was quite weakened. Tony's death was a shock for his older brother and so much for his sisters that they were unable to help their mother at all.

While the trauma of losing a son and brother in such an horrific way was difficult to take, subsequent court cases were even more difficult. Because of the way courtrooms are constructed there is little comfort for victims or their families. Throughout the depositions hearing, Joy Thomas had to share a waiting room with members of the local Mongrel Mob, patches and all. To say she felt intimidated would be an understatement. Thanks to the support of one particular woman, Joy was able to get through.

"Look them in the eye, she told me. I did it and it seemed to work, eventually they disappeared."

It seemed to go on forever, the court case. And sitting in the public foyer was far from enjoyable for an already traumatised victim. Around her were the parents, friends and supporters of three of the four people charged with Tony's murder. The fourth person was only 13 at the time. "There was so much we didn't know about what really happened," Joy recalled, "and the only way to find out was to go to the court case."

Joy Thomas' impression of the media was far from satisfactory.

"I was quite disgusted with them," she said.

"They didn't correctly report what was said in court. We heard one thing and read another!"

Tony had been stabbed in the heart with what was believed to be a sharpened screwdriver and for his death three accused were convicted of manslaughter. Two were sentenced to three years 11 months, while the other was imprisoned for three and a half years. All are now released yet what hurts Joy Thomas is she feels *she* has been sentenced to life.

That was not the only problem for the Thomas family. Like numerous other similar cases the pain doesn't end soon after the death

of a loved one. Neither does it get
easier having to battle through the
system. For some reason people
charged with murder, and their
supporters, often seem to regard it
as the victim's fault and to push the
blame on to them. Taunting, abuse
or harassment of the deceased's
family is commonplace and far more
common than most people would
believe.

Some two or three weeks after
Tony died, the label off the T-shirt
he was wearing at the time
mysteriously appeared on the back
lawn of the Thomas house. Just as
mysteriously the lights on Tony's
car were turned on one night. Tony's

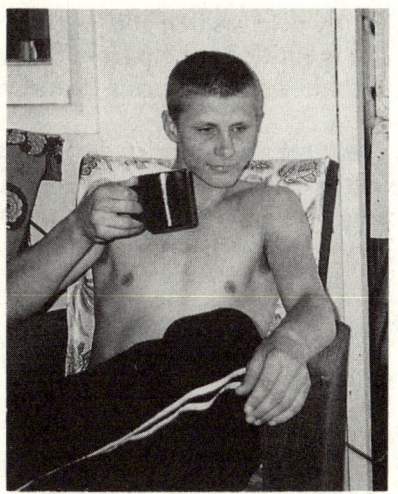

Tony Thomas.

12-year-old brother refused to go to school. His 11-year-old niece was
suspended from primary school for behavioural problems and Tony's
older brother never came home to stay again. The ripple effect of the
homicide began to take its toll on the family. Joy herself became
introverted and couldn't go into town for almost a year, believing
everyone was looking at her. Again this is a common belief among
the closest relatives of murder victims. Joy even kept a distance from
her own children, believing they too might be killed.

While Joy felt the police were good during the court case she was
not so praiseworthy of the justice system.

"We had to find out everything for ourselves," she said. "Even who
the prosecutor was. It was as if we weren't even there."

Joy's youngest son's attitude to life has changed completely. Even
after four years she is having problems with him. For 16 months or
more Joy Thomas slept with lights on. Where once she had never
locked doors, her house is now like Fort Knox.

With a son gone forever, Joy is bitter about the sentences the three
men got.

"They are free and all I have is a small casket of ashes and I still
cry and wake up at night when I think about what is called justice.
I can hear Tony calling to me, 'Mum, help me.' I have survived – I
wouldn't call it living, because most of me died when Tony did."

97

Joy believes that she, as the mother of a son killed by an unlawful act, is entitled to help from the ACC. "Physical injuries are one thing, but emotional suffering is forever."

The three men convicted of killing Joy Thomas' son have served their sentences. They received support throughout the proceedings and now they have 'paid' their debt to society. Joy Thomas still suffers from the effects and the support for her has been minimal.

12

Tammy Wilson

Sixteen-year-old Tammy Wilson was shot to death by a 46-year-old man she had run away to live with. On 23 October, 1987 he shot Tammy as he was "angry at himself for being angry with her." The couple had recently broken up after living together in Queenstown.

All too often the family of murder victims who are involved in investigations and subsequent trials feel themselves to be on trial. There is also a complete feeling of injustices that cast the spotlight off the offender and onto the victim.

The murder of Tammy Wilson is one such case. At the time of Tammy's death she was only 16 but her association with her murderer had been going on for some time. Numerous love letters between her and the 46-year-old man had been found, leaving Tammy's family in no doubt that she was infatuated with him. What disturbed them even more was his position of standing in the community and his responsibility as a school bus driver.

Suspicion about Tammy's liaison with the bus driver, Allan Sands, was first aroused when it was noticed how she was always home late from school and was the last passenger on the school bus. Suspicions were further aroused when Tammy was supposedly spending a weekend with a girlfriend. She was seen going down to the beach and when confronted made an excuse of going to meet a friend on a horse. But her story was far too complicated and she was followed. A short time later she was discovered in a campervan with Allan Sands, the man she was infatuated with, and who was to ultimately become her killer. When asked for an explanation Sands simply shrugged it off saying he was counselling her. Throwing the blame back at Tammy's parents he claimed they had 'filthy minds' and he was only sorting out all of Tammy's problems. Efforts to get help from school and Social Welfare proved fruitless and at one stage Tammy even turned up to a school dance with her companion, 30 years older than herself. A now distraught mother tried everything she could to end the relationship but to no avail.

Despite the pressure from her parents to end the relationship, Tammy was unable to and finally ran away with Sands, leaving Timaru and heading for a flat in Queenstown. But things didn't work out as a 16-year-old might expect and the relationship quickly soured. The man to whom she had become so devoted seemed less content with his young lover and sought the comforts of another woman and from there tensions escalated. While earlier in 1987 Tammy had seemed quite happy when visiting her mother, by the September she said her relationship with Sands had ended and she was now boarding with neighbours. She was even thinking of returning home later that year.

On the night of 23 October, 1987 a woman living in Queenstown answered her door to find Tammy in a very distressed state crying for help. Allan Sands was standing behind Tammy, completely naked.

"Help me, please help me," she cried. "Someone ring the police!"

An orange coat was given to Sands to make himself decent. As the girl was wrapped in a rug the neighbour was assured by Sands that he had called for the police and that they would be there soon.

The young girl could not accept comforting and each time Sands neared her she would cower away, continually repeating 'call the police, help me', and 'no, go away'. Although Sands remained composed and logical the young girl continued to be terrified. A teenage friend of Tammy's arrived and even she could not console the distressed girl. However she did notice injuries on Tammy's head and could see she had been crying for some time. At this stage Sands left but returned soon after, now dressed and returning the jacket to his neighbour. He insisted that he and Tammy talk in private until the police arrived, but as he had not rung for help the wait would be fruitless. While the girlfriend tried to make Sands leave she was told to 'shut up and get out.' Tammy assured her girlfriend she would be all right and she was left in a room with the door ajar. Within 30 seconds the door closed and she heard Tammy shout, "Don't come near me, get away," then scream out, "Hannah."

Immediately after the scream Hannah heard a loud bang as a .38 revolver was fired directly at Tammy's head. On opening the door Tammy's shocked teenage friend looked on at the sight before her. As she watched Sands said, "Goodbye babe," and shot himself. But the bullet merely grazed his forehead and after medical attention he was arrested. The rest is now history, but for Tammy's mother particularly, the resulting trials were to cause even more anguish. As she sees it the spotlight moved from where it should have been on the offender to her daughter whose life now came under scrutiny. Her thoughts follow...

I'll never forget the morning of 24 October, 1987. The police woke us at about 2.30am with the news of Tammy's death and we were to get to Queenstown to identify my daughter.

Tammy Wilson dressed for her school prom in 1986. The following year she was shot dead.

After letting family members know we left Timaru at 7.30am and got to Queenstown three hours later. We couldn't do anything until 2.00pm and waited outside the police station. Following that were the inevitable questions and statements.

I felt lost and very much alone, struggling to keep my feelings under control. I even felt guilty. I wanted to take Tammy back home for a funeral but her body had to go to Invercargill first for an autopsy. We stayed with friends at Cromwell, an hour out of Queenstown and they helped collect Tammy's possessions from the house where she had been boarding. From there we had the unenviable task of collecting Tammy's brother from Oamaru and explaining to relatives what had happened.

The undertaker couldn't have been more helpful and understanding as we waited four days for Tammy's body to be released. When we went to look at her I could hardly recognise her. She didn't look like my daughter and as I went to turn away I could see her fingernails with worn polish, but the unmistakeable colour I'd recognised from before. It was only then that I could realise it was Tammy. Her brother Paul said she looked like a princess but to me she looked so cold and very dead. I couldn't touch her and that was my worst experience, being unable to touch my own daughter one last time.

Tammy's funeral was quite big for one so young. We all have different ways of coping with death and my coping mechanism seemed to be alcohol. I wouldn't prescribe it for others but it seemed to help me at the time.

I had to be a witness at the preliminary hearing in Queenstown in January 1988 and travelled by rental car. I'm sure our older car wouldn't have made another trip there. We had got a letter saying we wouldn't be required after all as my evidence could be accepted in written form, but I still went. I wanted to know why. Needed to know why. We were unsure whether we would be allowed in the courtroom so sat with witnesses in the waiting room. It was then we saw Tammy's murderer arrive. He wasn't handcuffed and shook hands, kissed and spoke with others there. It looked for all the world to us as if he was turning up to court on a speeding charge. And that's how witnesses treated him. I sat through the proceedings but came home just as confused as ever.

In May 1988 the High Court trial was held in Invercargill and as I was a witness I would be required to give evidence. I was told what to expect and after giving my evidence sat listening to others. I sat and listened to how my 16-year-old ran to a neighbour's for help and how Sands followed her. How, when left alone, he shot my daughter then made a mess of trying to kill himself, if that's what he even intended. I then had to hear graphic evidence of how blood pumped from Tammy's head as though it were a fountain. How she screamed her friend's name before being shot.

Sands took the stand and talked of his impotence and how Tammy was always after him sexually. He told the court about a new car he had bought, a powder blue Mini, the mileage on the speedo and the condition it was in. I learned more about his damn car than his reason to murder. So much of his background didn't come out in court. Why did he have access to a revolver? Why was he living under an assumed name? What of his involvement with other people? Yet Tammy's young life was put under a microscope. From birth to death her life was made public but not his.

Our relief at the guilty verdict and a life sentence was tempered with the realisation of what life would mean. What he will serve in reality is far from a solid stand against murder. I will never forgive him for snatching Tammy from us. He just used her to boost his ego then cast her aside. Tammy was killed a little over a month short of her 17th birthday. She has gone but he still has a wife, a daughter and that damn car waiting for him. He'll probably be living less than 20 kilometres from me when he comes out. It's just too close.

I find it hard to express my true feelings especially trying to put it down on paper. At one stage I was even accused of having no feelings following the loss of Tammy. Tammy's father, my first husband, has told me he forgives the murderer. After the court case I wanted all this behind me but it's stupid comments like Tammy's father's that bring it all back. Then I have to explain why I can't forgive and I know I'll never forget. I don't want to forget.

13

Paul Anderson

Paul was a highly skilled lighting technician. On the night of Saturday, 2 May, 1992 he went to a Wellington nightclub to supply some equipment to a band. A patron who had been evicted by a doorman returned seeking revenge and, believing Paul worked for the nightclub, lunged at him with a knife causing fatal injuries.

The headline in Wellington's *Dominion* of Tuesday, 1 December 1992 seemed to say it all. "Witnesses tell of nightclub fight and fatal stabbing." That was how a Court report was headed up, detailing a "fight" between two men at the Carpark Rock Music Club in Wellington's Chews Lane. A "fight" that claimed the life of 25-year-old Paul Anderson, an innocent victim who was totally unaware of that earlier altercation.

With the number of murders in New Zealand during 1992 and the fact that this one happened in a nightclub, a sceptical public might, certainly on the superficial facts, be far from sympathetic. Many might ask, why was someone in a fight in a nightclub that was known to attract a rougher element. But if people were to only look behind the headlines they would realise that seven months before Graeme William Burton was convicted of murder, his victim was a totally innocent person simply in the wrong place at the wrong time.

Paul Anderson was one of Wellington's better known lighting technicians, highly skilled and highly respected. It was Paul who did the lighting for the Civic Centre opening in Wellington and the Royal New Zealand Ballet Festival production of *Orpheus*. Such was his expertise, Paul had been invited to provide lighting to a group at the prestigious Edinburgh Festival and was looking forward to travelling and working in Britain and on the Continent. However, Paul's life was suddenly ended at the hands of a drunken, drug-affected patron in the nightclub where Paul called in to supply some equipment to a band. Perhaps an obituary from Paul's friends at the Avalon Television Centre summed up how many felt about him.

OBITUARY

The lighting riggers at the Avalon Television Centre regretfully wish to note the death of Paul Anderson on the night of Saturday, 2 May 1992. Paul, a lighting technician, was employed by Grouse Lighting, a company which provides occasional rigging assistance to Avalon. Paul, aged 25 years, was well liked and respected by all those he worked with at Avalon and in Wellington's theatre and entertainment scene. He was renowned for his technical and artistic expertise, huge capacity for hard work, and his never ending cheerfulness. In the week before his death Paul had paid for and picked up his plane tickets for the big OE trip to New York at the end of the month. On Saturday Paul had been working in Avalon's Studio 8 rigging lights for *Wheel of Fortune* after that night's *Lotto* live draw. At 10.50pm he left Avalon to go to the Carpark Nightclub. As he was about to enter the club he was stabbed by a knife wielding patron who was being evicted. Paul was dead by 11.20pm before the ambulance could get him to hospital. His untimely death has saddened everyone in the Wellington theatre and entertainment community. He will be missed.

What actually happened was very much a case of someone being in the wrong place at the wrong time. Just before Paul Anderson had gone into the nightclub a patron, Burton, had been evicted by two doormen after one of them thought Burton had urinated on the floor by a pinball machine. The struggle at the door had been quite violent with a bottle being smashed over one of the bouncer's heads. Soon after Burton and his friends were forced outside, one of the doormen decided to leave the job immediately and went to get his coat when Burton came back with a knife screaming, "I'll kill him, I'll kill him." The man was intent on taking out his temper on anyone who worked at the nightclub. High on drugs and alcohol he was in no mood to reason. His enraged mind already affected by alcohol, Halcion (a sleeping pill), Valium (a tranquilliser) and the drugs LSD and cannabis along with the effects of magic mushrooms made Burton a dangerous person.

As Paul Anderson innocently walked into the club he was confronted by Burton who shouted, "Do you work here?" but he never waited for Paul to answer, instead stabbing him so violently in the chest the knife passed through the breastbone and into his heart. During the frenzied attack the victim was stabbed several more times in the chest and back before rolling with his attacker to the foot of the stairs. Within minutes Paul Anderson was dead and family and friends were left bewildered at how such a popular young man with so much to live for could have his life taken in such a violent way.

For Paul Anderson's family the morning after the fatal stabbing began in a devastating way. At 7.30 in the morning the police called to tell of Paul's tragic death and overnight a happy family of four had its plans and dreams shattered forever. Gone was the prospect of Paul's parents ever having the pleasure of being grandparents to their only son's children. Paul's sister's children will never have an uncle and the Anderson's only daughter, who had a close relationship with her brother will never again have a shoulder to lean on. These were some of the personal costs for a family of a murder victim.

The Andersons couldn't find the slightest fault in their treatment by either the Courts or the police. In fact they described the police they dealt with as being "the essence of kindness, attention and support throughout."

Recompense from the ACC covered approximately two-thirds of the funeral expenses but not the large amounts of expense from air fares to and from Wellington. Thanks to the generous assistance of friends further expenses for accommodation were not needed. Perhaps the thing that Paul Anderson's family finds hardest to come to grips with is the "justice" as they see it, of the murderer's future. As they say themselves, "Paul had an incredibly wide circle of friends and business associates, who from all accounts miss him as much as his family does. An intelligent, articulate young man, battling his way through life in these difficult times has had his life terminated by a thug who no doubt will be released by age 31. He will be able to live out the balance of his life but by any conservative estimate Paul's been deprived of at least 50 years. This is the "justice" system we live under as we approach the year 2000."

Since this story was written, Paul Anderson's father has made submissions to his local Member of Parliament, the Hon Clem Simich, asking for mandatory penalties for persons convicted of carrying offensive weapons such as knives, machetes and baseball bats in a public place. Mr Anderson believes that a mandatory penalty might hopefully act as a deterrent in such cases. Mr Simich chairs the Law and Order Committee. The submissions were fully and favourably considered but ample remedies were already written into the statutes. The efforts of the Hon Clem Simich and Minister of Justice Doug Graham were appreciated by the Anderson family.

14

Kim Shaw

In January 1986, a 27-year-old Glen Eden woman, Kim Shaw, was killed after being shot at close range with a pump action shotgun. Her de facto husband was arrested and charged with the murder, found guilty of manslaughter and served half of an 18-month sentence.

The parents, brother, sisters and other members of Kim Shaw's family have had to accept the verdict of the jury who found her de facto husband not guilty of her murder. But right from the start they felt excluded and believe, years on, that the judicial system treated them with contempt. Their list of grievances made the process of dealing with Kim's death, the court cases and subsequent verdict all the more difficult to cope with.

Even early in the enquiry there were difficulties. Dennis Shaw, Kim's father, had the unenviable task of identifying his daughter's body. With Kim having been shot in the head it made the task for Dennis more difficult and he still believes a distant relative could have been found to do the task.

The Shaws are also annoyed that it took too long for the accused's solicitor to sign a form releasing Kim's body for the funeral. Her burial was delayed by 11 days which, at a time when the family was in shock, made matters worse. More was to come.

About a week after the funeral, family members went to remove Kim's possessions from the flat. They were surprised when Kim's de facto walked down the path and ordered them to leave. They didn't know he had been allowed bail. One night he even turned up at the house of Mr and Mrs Shaw. Later, arrangements were made to collect personal effects with the de facto husband's lawyer present. All they got was a pre-packed suitcase and a few other possessions and told not to touch anything else. As they went through the unit the de facto's brother and sister followed making sure nothing else was taken.

Kim Shaw.

The Shaws are still bitter that the dispute over Kim's possessions was never resolved. Things the parents gave their daughter were never returned and to make it worse they watched the man responsible for her death driving her car around the area they live in.

All of these things just added to the trauma of trying to come to grips with their loss. But of the things that upset the Shaws the most, it was the court cases. Kim's sister and father found the impersonal nature of the court cases particularly difficult. Sister Ruth said, "You sit in court and almost feel you don't belong. It's as if it's nothing to do with you." To the family it was as if Kim was no longer a person but just a name on a piece of paper.

Kim's father feels the same. "It's really the police case," said Dennis Shaw. "And it's out of our hands."

This is a feeling a lot of families of murder victims get. The case is fought out between the prosecution and defence and many family members feel completely alienated and often unaware of what is going on. When Kim died the family were thrown into a situation no one was prepared for. While people can mentally prepare for a sudden loss in the family, perhaps to an accident or illness, murders produce their own set of complications. Few if any people prepare for such an event.

"I can remember one morning thinking, do we arrange the funeral or do the police do it?" Ruth was to say later. "It was as if we were lost." Ruth did praise the detective assigned to the family saying he was fabulous and right there all the time.

"But you still didn't really know what was going on," she said.

"We still felt powerless and very much on the outside trying to look in." For the Shaws the verdict and subsequent early release of the offender was compounded when they learned he had been getting home leave for weekends. They still have trouble coming to grips with the verdict of the jury. The facts of the case were fairly simple. The crown prosecutor was reported as having said in his opening address:

> Thomsen was found by a neighbour cradling the body of Edith Kim Shaw, who had died almost immediately from a neck wound caused by the shotgun blast. Thomsen, 43, denied murdering his de facto wife on 10 January when he appeared in the Henderson District Court. Opening the case for the prosecution, Mr Morris said evidence would show that when the shotgun was fired, the dead woman was only about 30cm from the defendant. Neighbours had heard raised voices coming from the couple's flat during an argument over their dogs the morning of the woman's death, he said. Thomsen gave two statements to the police, Mr Morris said. In the first he claimed Miss Shaw had suggested cleaning his gun. After ejecting what he thought were all the cartridges, he pulled the trigger, accidentally shooting the woman who was sitting on the couch next to him. Later Thomsen gave another statement saying the first was not true. During the day he had taken two of his dogs, both sick, to his brother's house where his brother shot them with a gun belonging to Miss Shaw, Thomsen told the police. When he got home he was "playing around" with the gun and pumped it twice. The second time it fired, close to the woman's face although he had not pulled the trigger.

(According to Kim's family the dogs were exhumed and examined but found to be in good health).

Evidence was reported as having been given that a firearm's expert said it was impossible for the gun to be set off accidentally as had been claimed. For the defence Thomsen's counsel, Paul Temm QC was reported as saying in his closing address to the jury:

> There was no motive for murder. Thomsen obviously loved his de facto wife and his behaviour was inconsistent with that of someone who had deliberately shot her. He cradled her bleeding body, saying 'don't die, don't die' Mr Temm told the jury. It could be that his firearm has a hidden vice of which he knew nothing. Thomsen was unfamiliar with the gun which he had only a couple of weeks before the incident. In that particular Winchester pump action shotgun model it was possible to fail to pull the bolt back far enough to eject all the cartridges, leaving it loaded and cocked. Thomsen's first statement was an attempt to explain why the gun exploded in his hands. Later he had pulled himself together and, when he spoke to a second officer, had a different approach.

This left the jury with a decision to make. Following a three-hour deliberation the accused was found not guilty of murder but guilty of manslaughter. The rest is history. Thomsen has served his time for the manslaughter of Kim Shaw. But to the parents, brother and sisters of Kim, along with others in the family, there are many unresolved issues which seem destined to remain that way.

In cases such as this, where the family often know the offender well, they can feel aggrieved even more when others involved in the trial have a different perception to them. As an example the Judge, at sentencing, made a remark about Thomsen showing remorse for what he had done. But the family didn't then, and still don't, share that view.

15

Carol Pye and Martin Crossley

On 22 February, 1983 Carol Pye, aged 28, and her companion Martin Crossley, 25, were shot and killed by an acquaintance. The killing, in the settlement of Titoki near Whangarei, was for no apparent reason. A homicide investigation began soon after Carol's three children discovered their mother's body on returning home from school.

If there is anything that is sure to rub salt into the wounds of murder victims' families it is the injustices of the 'system.' One such case began on 22 February, 1983 when a young couple were shot and killed by an acquaintance for no apparent reason. Twenty-eight-year-old Carol Pye had only recently been divorced and was living with her three young children in a house at Titoki near Whangarei. At the time Carol had a companion, Trevor Martin Crossley, three years her junior.

Robert Coachie Harris and his 17-year-old girlfriend had lived for a while with Carol Pye and Martin Crossley (a cousin of Harris). About three weeks before the fatal day, Harris and his girlfriend moved out but returned on 22 February to pick up some personal effects. With them, Harris took a .22 rifle allegedly to shoot some turkeys around the Titoki farmhouse. At some stage Harris accused his cousin of spreading rumours about his girlfriend but the suggestions were laughed off. In his statement reported in the *Northern Advocate*

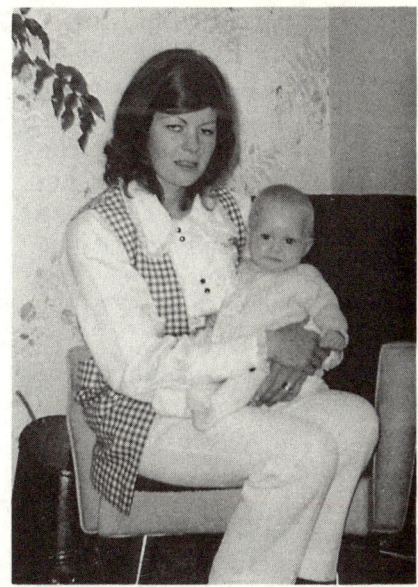

Carol Pye and her baby Michelle in 1972; Martin Crossley six months before he and Carol were killed.

during the trial, Harris was reported as saying, "...he went to walk away. I said something to him like, oh, you f... turkey and then I shot him in the back of the head, he fell forward on to the footpath."

At that stage Harris walked back to the house reloading the gun.

"I started calling out to Carol. When she came out and asked me what I wanted I said, come here, I want to show you something. When she went to walk past me I shot her in the back of the head. She didn't see Martin."

After the shooting Harris said he went around to the side of the house where his girlfriend asked him what he did and he told her to "shut up or she would be next." When Harris went back to the couple he is reported to have said in his statement, "I could see Carol was dead and Martin was still breathing. I was about 10-15 yards away and I shot him again in the head ... to put him out of his misery."

Before they left, Harris and a male accomplice (charged with being an accessory to the fact of murder), stripped marijuana leaves from plants Harris had grown and bagged them for sale. The 17-year-old girlfriend was given immunity from prosecution and gave evidence at the trial of being threatened by Harris not to tell the truth. During the trial she described the events of 22 February and said that on asking Harris why he did it, he answered, "it was just like having an ice cream."

For the seemingly unmotivated murders of Carol Pye and Martin Crossley, 35-year-old Harris was sentenced to life imprisonment. But the injustices and trauma for the family neither began nor ended with the trial and subsequent events were to plague both families for a long time. John Pye, estranged husband of Carol and father of her three children, felt that despite being only just divorced at the time of the murders, a very big part of his life was taken away.

"For the past decade I have kept silent hoping to rehabilitate the children from the trauma they went through when Carol died. They found their mother on the lawn when they came home from school that day. That was the start of the trauma for them."

"Although Carol and I had divorced I still loved her dearly and while I didn't want us to part, pressures forced it to happen. For the sake of the children we remained good friends despite the marriage breakup. Carol was very young when we met and perhaps we married for all the wrong reasons, but when she died I seemed to lose a big part of me. My children were so young at the time and for five years went through so much, mainly because of the system that plays into the hands of people who commit such terrible crimes. Throughout the investigation I felt that the children and I became the accused and the murderer was the victim. I couldn't understand why the police did deals for information with one of the people being given immunity from prosecution. A second man, originally charged along with Harris with the murders, had his charges replaced to being an accessory. During the trial my eldest daughter, then aged 10, had to give evidence. At one stage there was talk of a re-trial and there was no way I wanted my little girl going through that ordeal again. It was just so hard for her, having to give evidence at his trial. Nobody seems to consider the kids."

The trial didn't take place until November that year and John Pye considers that was far too long. Two "events" caused the trial to be delayed and one in particular was to have nationwide repercussions. While on remand at Auckland's Mount Eden Prison, Harris attempted to escape and was either pushed or fell from a prison wall. He injured a hip and ankle in the bungled attempt and the injuries meant a delay to the trial. That was not what infuriated the Pye and Crossley families. It was the compensation Harris got from the ACC that made them such disbelievers of the "system."

The three Pye children each received $500 put into trust until they reached 20. That was for the loss of their mother. Robert Harris received in excess of $18,000 for his injuries and to top it off his trial was paid for through legal aid. The furore over his payout caused major headlines and the ACC moved quickly to close the loophole. Had Harris been charged and convicted with escaping he could not have been paid out but the Corporation claimed they had no alternative but to pay, even though the claim came two years into Harris' sentence. Because of the injuries he suffered and the serious matters he was facing at the time, a charge of attempted escaping was not laid. Little could anyone envisage events that might follow some years later. Suggestions were made that Harris might put some of the payout into the trust fund for the murdered woman's children, a suggestion the children themselves found repugnant. In any event Harris never did set up any fund.

A second holdup to the trial occurred before Harris and his accomplice finally appeared. While it didn't attract the attention of the public it nevertheless annoyed John Pye.

"Harris had a girlfriend with him at the killings. She was pregnant and the trial was put off so she could have her baby. They didn't want her getting upset at the trial while carrying the baby. While it might have been hard on her, did anyone consider how hard it was on my kids? After all, who is the accused and who is the victim? Who should be considered first in these cases, the victim or the offender?"

John Pye's words are often being echoed by those who are quite clearly the victims locked into a system aimed at giving the offender a "fair go."

"When I consider what the children went through and comparing Harris' payout with what the youngsters got, it's a total injustice. The children and I had to completely change our lifestyles and it's taken a decade to get things into perspective. For all that happened to them the children have become well adjusted young adults. All credit to the children but no thanks to the system. My daughter is now 23 and recently married. My eldest son is 21 and went from being head boy at his college to begin teacher training, while the youngest at 19, is now a Waikato Polytechnic student."

The boys and their father recently went away on a music tour of the South Island. They are still all together after such an horrific episode in their lives.

But despite the efforts over a long time the costs have been considerable. The financial battles have been hard with the loss of their house, business and car. All of this can be, in part, directly attributable to the unfair things that happened since that fateful day in February 1983.

For the Crossley family the loss of their son was every bit as traumatic. They cannot replace their son and believe that for a cold, calculated murder life should mean life. They, like the Pyes, were left to pick up the financial and emotional pieces.

Martin's mother Billie has seen the injustices in the system, and after 12 years is still very resentful. To her the injustices seem worse than the dreadful tragedy itself.

When a local policeman told us our son had been shot we wanted to know the details. We had to know. But no one could tell us, even at the police station. We eventually heard what we wanted to know on the radio. That was a terrible shock and started the tears and heartache all over again. We even wanted to go to the scene but were told it was cordoned off. I wanted to identify my son but wasn't allowed to as someone had already done that. God knows who, for I don't.

The trials of Harris were particularly frustrating for us. The High Court trial was to be held in Whangarei on 13 June and was scheduled to last at least a week. We live in a small Waikato town where we owned our business. Arrangements were made for someone to take over the business while we were away. As it is a 3 1/2 hour drive to Whangarei we got up early, packed and dressed ready to depart. A phone call came just before we were to leave to say the trial was postponed.

This left us upset and angry. Our first response was why? We were never given any real explanation. The next scheduled date was 12 September. We had no power over the situation and felt empty. There was just nothing we could do to make things happen.

During the period June-September we arranged to sell our business. We wanted to be free for the trial believing it was more important to us than anything else at the time. A buyer was found and after some negotiation we were free to attend our son's murderer's trial. We headed for my sister's home at Hikurangi the day before the trial en route to Whangarei but the next morning we got a phone call to say the trial was yet again postponed. Harris, on attempting to escape from prison had broken his leg and was in hospital.

The whole thing was now starting to seem like a bizarre serial. We were now angry and frustrated. The system was out of our control and after staying another day with my sister we returned to the Waikato to await the next date.

Still hoping for a date later in September we were told that wasn't possible. The accused's 17-year-old de facto wife was expecting a baby. (She was eventually to give evidence for the prosecution). Our frustration wasn't just with the postponements and the dates, but rather the fact that all the considerations seemed to be for the one who had caused the situation, not the victims. Finally in November the trial went ahead.

The ACC farce of Harris getting over $18,000 compensation when he broke his leg was sickening. Carol's children got $500 on turning 20 and we got $100 towards Martin's funeral expenses. What an insult. Since that was allowed to happen I have never had any faith in the system.

As if all of this wasn't enough, worse was to happen that piled misery and unhappiness on to us. In June 1992 my husband Trevor died suddenly. He had never been able to accept the way Martin died. Had it been an accident, perhaps his acceptance would be easier but not the terrible way Martin died, unable to defend himself or Carol. I truly believe Trevor died of a broken heart. We had previously lost two infant children, one older than Martin and one younger. This final loss, in such a brutal and unnecessary way had really devastated my husband. Of four children and a husband in my family I now have a daughter left.

What did the system do? It found a man guilty of murder and sentenced him to life in prison. After nine years it released him. It gave him over $18,000 for an injury suffered while trying to escape from prison. He got a lump sum for pain and suffering and loss of enjoyment of life. Loss of enjoyment of life in Paremoremo!! A system that continues to pay him a sickness benefit.

Is it any wonder I feel bitter? Is it any wonder I have no faith in the system? My son was murdered but who really gets the "life" sentence?

Perhaps the ultimate irony of all happened in December 1992 when Robert Harris was released from prison after serving only nine years *of a life sentence. And just two years later he was to again feature in the news after breaking a man's jaw in a hotel altercation during a drinking session. While he could have been recalled to finish his "life" sentence he was instead convicted and ordered to pay $1,600 in reparation to his victim.*

16

Dean Willis

A simple request for a cigarette was enough provocation for two men to beat Dean Willis to death. On 27 June, 1992 he was attacked, dragged by his heels through an alleyway into a schoolground and severely beaten again. He died from the injuries and was discovered the next morning by boys crossing through the school.

The day before Dean Willis was murdered he had sold his house in Rotorua. He was excited at the prospect of returning to Perth where he could live near his seven-year-old son. Dean had crossed the Tasman to New Zealand a year before but had desperately missed seeing his son. Saturday, 27 June, 1992 was a chance for Dean to say goodbye to his friends over a few drinks in a local hotel. He would then return to his mother's to stay a few days before flying to Australia.

Dean Willis was in a jovial mood, excited at the prospects ahead and it would be fair to say he probably overdid the celebrating. Not that he in any way became aggressive or obnoxious. On the contrary he remained jovial and friendly but quite defenceless.

A doorman suggested to Dean that perhaps it was time he went home and rang a taxi. Dean waited on the verandah by the lounge but unfortunately, also waiting in the same place were two young men, both disgruntled after having been refused admission to the lounge because of their dress. While Dean Willis leant against the wall an eyewitness saw one of the men hit Dean in the face. Soon after, the doorman intervened when he saw Dean pushed down the steps, telling the two assailants to pick on someone who could defend themselves.

At that point Dean Willis wandered to a nearby service station on Fairy Springs Road where he tried to buy a packet of cigarettes. He had spent all of his cash at the hotel and the garage assistant rang another taxi to pick Dean up. Dean told the assistant he had money, showing a receipt of the house sale, though clearly he had no cash on him. The assailants had by this time also crossed the road to the service station and may well have heard Dean talking about having sold a house. On leaving the garage to wait for the taxi it is most likely Dean failed to recognise the two men and a young woman waiting outside, as the assailants of a few minutes before. He asked them for a cigarette. Soon after a vicious assault was to take place that left Dean Willis alone in a nearby schoolground fighting for his life.

A woman reported seeing Dean lying curled up on the grass verge being kicked in the head as another male and female stood by watching. Fairy Springs Road is very busy and almost certainly others would have seen the attack yet no one stopped to help. Perhaps it is an indictment on our society and our acceptance of violence that help was not sought at that time.

The two men then supported Dean with his arms around their necks as they carried him 100 metres down Ferguson Place. After dropping him to the ground they then reigned punches and kicks onto their injured and defenceless victim. From there they dragged him by his ankles down an asphalt road and alleyway, a distance of about 300 metres, stopping briefly to assault him again before taking his wallet. From there they dragged him across a stream, up a slope and through a wire fence to the high school grounds.

Despite the injuries already inflicted by the kicks and punches and the severe grazing caused by the dragging, Dean was finally stripped as he was pulled through a fence, kicked in the head and body yet again then, as a final gesture, stomped on the chest.

Dean Willis was not dead when he was left alone, but his injuries included several broken ribs, a punctured lung, severe bruising and lacerations and a brain haemorrhage which would have required surgery to keep him alive. Over 40% of Dean's skin was removed from his back, buttocks and elbows caused by the rough road surface as he was dragged by the heels. When the assailants left him his tracksuit pants were down to his knees while the upper clothing had been removed. The night of 27 June was one of Rotorua's coldest that winter. Being left in the freezing cold with such massive injuries, Dean Willis had virtually no chance of surviving.

When Dean Willis died his family suffered through a series of mishaps that made the event more traumatic than it should have been. While many of the issues were resolved so that in future cases what happened to the Willis family would not happen to others, one issue remains unresolved. Dean's sister

Dean Willis with his son Shane several years before Dean's death.

Raewyn is concerned that this issue, what she calls media insensitivity, will affect other families as it did hers.

At the time Dean Willis was found it was quite obvious, even to the boys who stumbled across the scene that he was dead. A homicide investigation began immediately. To preserve the scene police, as they do in all such cases, leave things as undisturbed as possible. Normally a tent or other such covering is used to protect the scene, not only from weather and other interference but also from prying eyes. In this case that was not done and on the Monday a photograph of Dean's partly clothed body was shown on the front page of Rotorua's *Daily Post* newspaper. The family, in shocked disbelief at what they were seeing, felt this to be intrusive and not allowing Dean's dignity to be preserved. Worse was to come. The television news also showed the scene.

Raewyn Willis complained to the police, to the Press Council and the Broadcasting Standards Authority. To their credit the police district commander acknowledged Raewyn's concerns about a deceased's dignity being preserved and the need for privacy screens to be erected to keep out intrusive media lenses. Steps were immediately put into place to consider this in future. A senior officer who had not

121

been part of the enquiry visited Raewyn and her mother and went through the various issues, a gesture they appreciated.

The response from the Press Council was simple. Raewyn's complaint was out of the time-frame in which they would do anything. Besides she would have to take the issues up with the paper first if any formal complaint was to be lodged. The Press Council did seek an explanation from the paper but reiterated that due to the time gap between publication and the complaint the Council would not conduct an investigation. In a letter to Raewyn they said they hoped the editor's response to the Council would go some way to address her concerns. It did not.

As far as Raewyn was concerned time meant nothing. She had been unable to bring herself to write about the situation any earlier, which is hardly surprising when one realises the brutal nature of her brother's death. In any event she wasn't even aware the Press Council existed until someone told her, let alone there was a time limit on complaints. The reply from the newspaper literally justified their actions but to Raewyn's mind it just was not an acceptable practice. She strongly feels with others who have murder invade their family that the last thing they want are pictures of their loved ones splashed across papers and television screens reflecting the indignity such deaths portray.

One of the problems with such a case as this is that the photographs or video footage become archival. Dean Willis was killed on 27 June, 1992. A programme about someone related to one of those charged with his murder was screened on a *Holmes* programme and showed Dean's body lying in the school grounds. This programme screened on 2 February, 1994. Had this been shown in connection with Dean's death it would have been difficult enough, but in an unrelated story it was very distressing despite the programme producer believing what they were showing had some relevance.

Such are the difficulties families face with the media and in cases of murder they can be excessive. Raewyn Willis complained to the *Holmes* show and in a reply the producer acknowledged the victim's perspective was not given the thought it should have. All the same it had still been screened and caused distress to the family.

Of the investigation and trials Raewyn had some personal thoughts. Things she felt were not right and she would like to see changed for future cases:

While at the time I was disappointed at the lack of dignity police showed to Dean while he was at the school and the lack of information about the early stages of the investigation, in other ways they were very good. Since Dean's death the police have acknowledged more privacy should have been provided and in future that will be done, but I believe there needs to be better training for police who let families know about such deaths as Dean's. We felt interrogated before we were told Dean was dead. The way we were asked the questions put me on the defensive because I thought Dean had done something wrong. My niece and nephew, aged 7 and 9 were in an adjoining room and could hear every word spoken. It would have been prudent if the detective had given us the opportunity to ensure more privacy. As I took the children next door they asked me if Uncle Dean was dead but what do you say at times like that? I was in shock and as we did not identify him until later that day I remained unconvinced he was dead so I told the children he was injured.

Results of a post-mortem should be given to the family personally. We knew Dean was dead but not how he died and heard this on the television news at 6.00pm. I rang the police station and was told a bit more information though at times like that it is hard to comprehend over the phone. The cause of death was a combination of the injuries and hypothermia though the impression the television news item gave it was the cold that was the cause of death. It is much the same with other parts of the investigation where we felt unsure of what was going on. At those times you start to listen to and believe some of the gossip that goes on in the town.

We believe that there should be more sensitivity in court cases. I know and appreciate that defence counsel have a job to do for their client, but why can't they be a bit more sensitive? For example, Mr Mike Bungay during his summing up to the jury held up a picture of Dean's bruised and battered head. He didn't just direct it to the jury. He flashed it around to the spectators in the gallery which included our family. The jury had the photos so he didn't need to hold one up other than for impact. We had been offered the chance to see the photographs of Dean but chose not to. I thought it was heartless of Mr Bungay to do what he did and I was angry because it upset Mum so much.

I was going to write to Mr Bungay but he died soon after this trial. A lawyer at Citizens' Advice told us Mr Bungay would probably have said if we didn't want to see something that upset us we shouldn't be there. But why shouldn't we? It was a member of our family who was killed.

I also believe that intimidating-looking people shouldn't be allowed in court when certain people are giving evidence. I am sure people don't tell the truth when this happens. I also feel strongly that victims' families should have a separate room in which to wait during a trial. It is very stressful having to sit in a room full of witnesses, especially if some are friends or relatives of those on trial.

It is also very hard having defendants sitting just a few feet in front of you at the trial (I sometimes felt like reaching out and hitting them). Court rooms are going to have to be better designed to separate defendants from the families.

I have already talked about my views of the media but perhaps a plea to television, not just for us but many other families. If you have to use footage taken some time before, have the decency to tell the family beforehand. It's very distressing to watch television about something unrelated and see your loved one's body on the screen. That's very distressing and just raises all the nightmares again. Please be a bit more sensitive.

And my final thoughts were about the verdicts. It seems to me that one assailant was found guilty of murder while the other was guilty of manslaughter because a crucial factor was not presented to the jury. It related to the footwear worn by one of the two assailants. Perhaps the following extract from the *Daily Post* on Saturday, 19 December, 1992 will sum up what happened to Dean and some of our frustrations at the final result.

Boots May Have Done Most Damage: Judge –
The footwear of a Rotorua youth found guilty of the manslaughter of Dean Mark Willis, was more consistent with having inflicted the more serious injuries suffered by the deceased than that of his co-accused who was found guilty of murder, Mr Justice Doogue said in the High Court at Rotorua yesterday.

He sentenced 16-year-old Jason Rajoo Ralm who was recently found not guilty of murder, but guilty of manslaughter, to 8 1/2 years jail. Thirty-five-year-old Mr Willis was found dead, half-naked and beaten, in a field at Western Heights High School on 28 June this year. He was found to have suffered severe bruising, head and chest injuries, and three broken ribs. He had lost about 40 percent of his skin, consistent with his having been dragged by the heels over a considerable distance.

He had also suffered from hypothermia.

In sentencing Ralm yesterday, Mr Justice Doogue described the beating as wanton, brutal injuring. In finding Mahia guilty of murder and Ralm of manslaughter, the jury must have taken the view that Mahia had been the principal assailant and that he had known death was likely as a result of the injuries being inflicted on Mr Willis.

'The jury must also have found that your part was not as great and that, because of your lesser age and intoxication at the time, you may not have known death was a possible consequence of the injuries being inflicted,' His Honour said.

It had been put to the jury that Ralm was wearing gumboots at the time of the beating. They may not have realised, as the Crown did not raise it, that the gumboots had been steel-capped and were likely to have caused the most serious injuries. There had been references during the trial to Mahia wearing ordinary shoes, said His Honour. The injuries inflicted by both youths had been deliberate and both had been reckless as to what happened to Mr Willis...

Raewyn Willis feels strongly that for justice to be done in crimes such as the murder that affected her family some things have to change. Although she found the police were sensitive and couldn't be nicer during the investigation there were things that should have been done to ease the trauma. While Dean's death, investigation, court cases etc are all over, her experiences have led to her hoping that by explaining these effects it might ease others' pain when they are facing the terrible stresses murders create.

Since Dean's tragic death numerous initiatives have been put in place that address some of Raewyn Willis' concerns. Victim support groups now have trained homicide volunteers who get called in at the early stages of the murder enquiry. They liaise closely with the investigation team and the family. A Justice Department initiative has provided for victims court assistants. These people liaise directly with victims and provide information, emotional support and a raft of other needs victims find necessary during the court process. Both of these victim-orientated initiatives have made a considerable difference to easing the burden on families faced with such horrific ordeals.

17

Keith Cochrane

Keith Cochrane died in Waikato Hospital on 20 November, 1987. He had been brought to the hospital after being bound, beaten and burned at a gang house in Hamilton. Seven men were found guilty of Keith's torture and subsequent death.

Keith Cochrane and fiancee Carolyn Jackson had a stable, long lasting relationship. Although they had only recently decided to marry the couple had been together for five years. With a job for Keith waiting in Australia things looked bright for the couple and within days he was to head across the Tasman. After finding accommodation, Carolyn would follow and together they would set up home in their newly adopted country.

But things didn't go to plan. On 19 November, 1987, Carolyn was at home with a girlfriend watching television. The two young women were discussing Carolyn's wedding plans and talking about her future in Australia.

The phone call Carolyn answered suddenly changed everything. Keith was in the hospital having been beaten. The two women went direct to the Waikato Hospital fully expecting to bring him home, but rather than being taken to the Accident & Emergency Department, Carolyn was ushered into the Intensive Care Unit. As she went in, Keith's parents and sister were coming out, in shock and crying.

"Carolyn, he's really bad," Keith's sister said.

"I rushed into the room and was unable to recognise the man I loved," said a disbelieving Carolyn. "I just wanted to put my arms around him, but all over his body were slashes, cigarette burns and gaping wounds held together with stitches. A nurse gave me a chair and I started to gently rub him, pleading with him not to leave me."

Carolyn stayed with Keith for hours and remembers vividly the monitor and tubes all over the man she was about to marry.

When the police arrived Carolyn was ushered into a room and asked if she could shed any light on to who might be responsible for Keith's beating, or why. It was while she was being interviewed that she could hear or sense the monitor on Keith

Keith Cochrane.

stop. She knew instantly that Keith's life had ended. In a blind panic she rushed back to him, held his hand, not wanting him to go. But for the couple it was too late.

For Keith's parents and sister the shock was just as profound. After receiving a call from the police to say their son and brother was in Waikato Hospital, little did they know that the call was to begin a nightmare that seemingly has no end. They, like Carolyn, imagined Keith would have cuts and bruises and on the way to the hospital his mother recalls being angry at him.

"He was to start a new job in Australia in a few days, so why end up in such a situation now." On being taken into intensive care such thoughts quickly disappeared. The shock of what they were to see will never leave them. On looking around the ward they couldn't recognise Keith – a mother couldn't even recognise her own son.

"Keith's face was like raw meat," Pam Cochrane recalls of being at her son's bedside. "He had been beaten with wood, stabbed, had cigarette burns over his body and not only were his legs broken, but so too were his fingers after having been bent backwards. On his ankles were rope burns where Keith had been tied up."

The young man's parents and sister couldn't even touch him for fear of hurting him further, despite the fact he was unconscious. Keith Cochrane died 20 hours later from a massive brain haemorrhage caused by the steel capped boots that were used to repeatedly kick him in the head.

Immediately after Keith's death, Carolyn left the hospital in a blind panic just wanting to get away. She found a phone booth across from the hospital, but looking through tears was unable to focus on the number she wanted. Through the kindness of a passing lady, Carolyn was taken home where she went into her room, wrapped herself in Keith's jacket with thoughts that this was all she had left of the man she loved. For a long time, that jacket was never to be out of Carolyn's sight.

Before Carolyn had met Keith she had a daughter and recalls how Keith was the only father her little girl ever knew.

"They adored one another," she said, "and he treated her as though she were his own."

"I sat down and wrote a letter to Keith and Annalisa drew him a picture. She was too young to understand what had happened." The following day Carolyn went to the funeral home to bid farewell to Keith, placed the letter, her daughter's drawing and their engagement ring in the coffin and left. To Carolyn the funeral was mostly a blur. She didn't really know what was going on and didn't want to believe it anyway.

The immediate days after Keith's death were no less easy on the Cochranes. Thoughts of what happened, who did it, and why flooded through their minds. Numerous calls came, one in particular from some young men claiming to be Keith's friends. They asked if they could attend the funeral, Mrs Cochrane recalled.

"We thought it was a lovely gesture and they brought with them two of the largest wreaths of flowers I've ever seen." After the service they asked if they could fill in the grave, something Mrs Cochrane was happy to let them do. Soon after, she cursed the day she let them have anything to do with the final farewell to her son. On 3 December, 1987 those seven men were arrested for the death of Keith Cochrane.

"There were seven of them that killed Keith," Mrs Cochrane said, "seven to one, Keith never stood a chance."

Keith Cochrane had been taken to Waikato Hospital in a car used

128

by two of those to be charged with his death. Not only had he been severely beaten but, the Crown alleged at the trial, he had been tortured. While bound he was savagely and sadistically beaten with lumps of wood, boots and fists, stabbed and slashed with a knife and burned with cigarettes on the hands. It was unclear how long Keith was held captive but it could have been for several days. Why such a savage attack should be made was unclear as was Keith Cochrane's silence. Although critically injured and often only semi-conscious, he would not say who administered what would soon prove to be fatal injuries. When police pleaded with him to say who inflicted the injuries he simply replied, "No one."

Mrs Cochrane is bitter about the senseless killing of her son and about the system she sees as being there to protect us. But to her that is far from what it seems. The seven were charged with manslaughter.

"Why not murder?" she asked, but was told that with seven of them sticking together the chances of a murder conviction being proven were remote and that all could walk free. Although it might seem logical to charge all seven jointly, Pam Cochrane wanted to know why they couldn't be tried separately. The answer that it would cost too much, while being a reality, brought home to her the realisation that her son's life now came down to dollars and cents.

After a High Court trial lasting three and a half weeks the jury was unable to agree and a second trial had to be held adding considerable trauma to the family. Following another two and a half weeks of a High Court trial the jury returned a verdict of guilty but it was far from over yet. For the brutal killing of Keith Cochrane, seven were sentenced to terms of imprisonment ranging from two to six years. The Crown appealed on the grounds that the sentences were inadequate and the Court of Appeal increased the penalties to six years but in Pam Cochrane's mind this was still far from enough. When she balances the accused's benefits to those of her family she gets angry.

"Lawyers were supplied to each of them, all on legal aid. Their fees alone would have been phenomenal."

The depositions, two High Court trials and a Court of Appeal hearing took two years to complete and when one thinks of the expenses involving judges, witnesses and other costs bringing the matter to a conclusion, it was indeed expensive.

Pam Cochrane still believes that costs would have been no higher had the charges been tried separately and perhaps the reasons why Keith died might have been told. Even now the family still don't know why. And why seems to be the common question the victims left behind in homicide cases always ask.

One might imagine that losing a loved one the way Keith died, the trauma of the funeral and subsequent Court cases, all of the attached media interest would be enough, but not in this case. For a long time, Keith's fiancee couldn't sleep and then when she did her sleep was punctuated with nightmares at the way her husband-to-be looked just before he died. She began to drink heavily, by herself and sometimes all night catching up with sleep during the day. Luckily her mother was able to look after Annalisa. With a feeling of desperation surrounding her, Carolyn decided the only way out of her nightmare was suicide, and taking a bottle of pills seemed the only solution. Although she didn't think so at the time, luck was on her side and the pills, rather than cause her to escape her situation, only made her sick. On recovery she returned home to further nightmares, strained relationships at home and with others. Carolyn realised family and friends were there but they couldn't help her, she wouldn't let them.

"My life had been shattered," she said, "I just wanted to be alone." Unable to settle down, Carolyn shifted from house to house. Occasionally she would go out on dates but they never lasted. Often she would find excuses to go out to the cemetery and remain there, often late at night alone with her thoughts and tears.

It is easy for people to say you should pull yourself together and get on with life. Those who have any understanding of how death affects people know that grief has a different way of manifesting itself in us. Losing a loved one is always traumatic but under the circumstances such as the way Keith Cochrane died, it is little wonder that his fiancee, a woman he had lived with for five years and with whom he had built plans for the future, would be affected the way she was. Even seven years after Keith's death, Carolyn has difficulty letting anyone close to her.

"There is a place in my heart where no-one else will enter. My outlook on life has changed and I know that I will live with a ghost for the rest of my days."

Homicides such as the one that claimed Keith's life have a profound effect on many people. And, though it might be hard to believe, victims, i.e. the family and friends of the deceased, are often subjected to what is little short of cruelty. Publicity and the stares of some and avoidance by others is to be expected though it doesn't make life any more bearable. In the case of the Cochranes, pressure went on them that was not only cruel but quite obscene. Keith's older sister, who had visited the hospital and saw the horrific injuries, was subjected to harassment by associates of the offenders. They followed her down the street chanting, "Keith Cochrane is dead, dead, dead," She was threatened and even spat on, and she was the victim! Unable to take it any more she left New Zealand and went overseas and though she will never be able to erase the horror of her brother's death, she has been able to find some happiness there.

Pam Cochrane accepts that her daughter had to go overseas to escape the torment, but even realising the necessity she questions why.

"Why should she have to go? She's done nothing wrong." Not only have the Cochranes lost their son but also a daughter and all because of the actions of someone else. In cases of homicide the circle of victims is certainly wide. Keith's younger sister is now growing up but her parents worry. They feared for her and whenever she went out someone was always with her.

"Living in the same city as Keith's killers, all of whom are now released, we felt vulnerable and that's why we wouldn't let her alone in town." The youngest daughter has now left Hamilton, unable to live with the pressures of the past.

Out of this terrible tragedy, Pam Cochrane has gained some strength. Strength she says to fight against the system, particularly the Accident Compensation Corporation for the rights of every murder victim's family. Pam and her family feel they have been neglected and let down by the system.

"Anything I wanted to know, I had to get from the Ombudsman," she said. "Once Keith's killers were arrested that seemed to be the end of the information we needed, information that might have answered the questions we had. If only we had been told what was going on instead of reading it in the papers or hearing it on the streets." Even sitting through Court cases failed to give them the answers they so desperately needed.

At the time of Keith's death his mother worked at the hospital and as each day got harder, she left and took up a job in a factory. With family commitments there was no alternative but to work.

"As a family we nearly destroyed each other," she recalled. "We would keep going over Keith's killing, time and time again and always blaming ourselves." At this vulnerable time the Cochranes felt very much alone. A claim to ACC for 'extreme emotional trauma' which might have paid for much-needed counselling, was turned down.

"I couldn't believe their reply," Pam Cochrane said. "Because you did not witness your son's killing or have a physical wound, you do not qualify for a payment," was the reply that made Pam Cochrane angry. Does one have to witness a killing to be affected she might well ask.

At an ACC review, salt was rubbed further into the wounds when she was told that had her son fought back and wounded any of his attackers, they would have been able to make a claim. By now nothing was making sense. The injustices for the victims was incredible. If only the family and Keith's fiancee could have been given counselling of some sort they believe the terrible effects of this crime could have been minimised.

"Everything was presented to our son's killers on a plate," Mrs Cochrane said. "They could get legal aid, counsellors and seemingly whatever they wanted, but we couldn't get a thing." The Cochranes believe that in such cases there should be a Court-appointed lawyer to help people through. They found it hard sitting in Court knowing things said were simply untrue yet being unable to say a word. Even now, some seven years after the tragic events unfolded the family is fragile.

"The pain never goes away and nights are always the worst. It only takes a little thing to bring it all back to us, a particular song on the radio, a young man passing by with blond hair, so many things. I think of the daughter-in-law I'll never have, grandchildren that will never be. I still have visions of Keith being tied up and beaten with no one there to help him. I can still hear the laughter and cheers from Keith's killers when they were found guilty."

Pam Cochrane says she hates the seven men who killed her son and she has good reason to. She often asks what right did they have to kill Keith and destroy her family. When one thinks of the devastation others have caused to a close-knit happy family then perhaps she is well justified in her beliefs. Pam's final words on the subject sum up what this has meant for her and the family.

"*I get so upset when I visit Keith's grave. He will always remain there but now his killers walk free.*"

18

Alan Field

On 30 July, 1992 Alan Field drove to a pre-arranged business meeting with an associate. When he got out of his car he was shot seven times by the associate who was later imprisoned for life for Alan's murder.

If anyone should doubt the effects a murder has on those closest to a victim then Linda Field's experiences should dispel any misconceptions. With ten years of legal secretarial experience behind her, none of that prepared her in any way for what she and her family went through. These are her feelings, not about the murder, but rather the effects nearly a year later.

Before starting let me say how well we were supported by the police and victim support volunteers. Not only did they show understanding and compassion, but the volunteers provided constant and genuine support through the whole ordeal.

Let me now recount the trial. It was set down some 11 months after the murder which we all found pretty hard to take. I couldn't understand why it took so long where other trials have occurred within a few months of the incident. It becomes difficult to "get on" with our lives until the trial is finally over. Imagine having to re-live the circumstances a year later. All it does is send you back to the beginning again. I had made tremendous inroads into dealing with what had happened so believed I was well prepared for the trial. Two weeks prior to the trial I went with victim support volunteers to view the various High Court rooms that might be used for my late husband's trial. My first impressions were how small they were. "Do we all sit together?" was my first question. It's hard to imagine the victim's family having to sit throughout the length of a trial together with the family of a man you know killed your husband in cold blood.

I could remember the depositions hearing in the District Court on Auckland's North Shore. The waiting room facilities there were far more conducive to privacy for all the parties concerned. At least areas were partitioned off so our family could sit in one corner and they in another. While they might have heard me when I broke down at least they couldn't witness the event. So experiencing a degree of privacy on the North Shore I thought the new, supposedly fabulous High Court of Auckland, would have been built with victims' families in mind. My visit to the High Court showed me this was clearly not the case. The seating outside the various court rooms was all in open spaces with no privacy available. Witnesses, for and against, were literally seated side by side.

Alan was a very popular and loved guy so naturally all of his family and mine wanted to attend as support and for their own reasons. So too did his many friends. The seating in the first court room on day one was inadequate to the extent the judge ordered a new court room be made available but this was still unsuitable. People ended up having to "fight" over a seat and getting there early was a priority. At one stage there were so many people in the gallery there wasn't even a seat left for the accused's wife who arrived a few minutes late. The judge had to direct someone to leave the gallery to give up a seat for her. It was an awful experience to go through for her and for me. As if it's not bad enough having to attend your husband's trial without having the embarrassment of trying to find a seat.

The trial started and there, to my astonishment, is my husband's murderer some two or three metres from me. He never stood in the dock until the jury returned with its verdict of guilty. He had instead been seated beside his counsel, paid for of course by legal aid. We had a competent Crown Prosecutor who we believed did an excellent job. But to us it seemed incomprehensible a man charged with murder, on legal aid, can get a Queen's Counsel for his representation.

During the trial the accused was given copies of all the court documents and police photographs. The photos of his handiwork, my husband's body lying on the footpath with seven bullets in him.

What I wanted was to have the man in the dock facing the gallery, not with his back to us. Let him see how many lives his actions have affected. His family, his children, me and all my family and friends, Alan's closest buddies. What have they lost? I wanted him to face us, to see me crying.

I didn't feel anger, not at the time, but that changed when the verdict was read out. We had gone through so much hurt, stress and fear. Yes, fear that the jury would agree with the defence argument that it was manslaughter. I couldn't understand how a man could admit killing another, yet plead not guilty and have a defence of

Alan Field.

manslaughter. There was no opposition by the defence to the fact the accused killed Alan, yet somehow their business relationship warranted Alan being shot as he got out of his car for a prearranged meeting. Words weren't even exchanged before Alan was shot first, then twice more as he tried to flee. As Alan hadn't died instantly three more shots were fired killing him. The coroner's findings were that after the sixth shot Alan had died, yet the accused shot him a seventh time, in the back of the neck. Alan was an unarmed man shot once in the front of the shoulder and six times in the back.

The accused rang the police and gave himself up which fortunately meant we did not have to go through the anguish of a long investigation waiting to hear who killed Alan. That way we were saved from experiencing the invasion by the media during our grieving, unlike so many other families when these high profile violent crimes affect them. But we had to go through the anguish of nearly a year and the expense to the State of a week-long trial to prove something we all knew – that he was guilty of murder.

The only good thing I can say about the whole trial was that he was sentenced there and then. We didn't have to go through another wait for the sentencing.

Life imprisonment is the mandatory sentence for murder. To the layman that might seem an adequate punishment but how many are aware of the parole provisions? We were told the accused would quite probably be regarded as a "model" prisoner and therefore eligible for parole after about 10 years. Do I get my life back the way it was in 10 years' time? Do I get the chance to have the child I wanted with Alan? Do Alan's friends and family get him back in 10 years' time to enjoy the rest of their lives with him?

This all reads pretty emotional but the murderer and society needs to be aware of the costs. It's not just Alan's life that was taken by an act of violence. Think of all the other lives that are affected.

And what of the repercussions for the murderer? There's no real fear of the consequences. As far as I'm concerned he now has a roof over his head, he receives an allowance, further education and job opportunities, no responsibilities, family or business hassles and literally no stress. His business partner and wife have those problems to contend with but not him.

However those of us on the "outside" have all of those problems but worse because we are the ones who lost a loved one who helped us with all those problems. In 10 years' time he, the offender, can pick up the threads of his life and start over while we in society are expected to open our arms after 10 years and say "yes, you've served your time, welcome back!"

Personally I believe the only deterrent against violent, premeditated murder is the death penalty. Also if degrees of murder were introduced it would allow juries to recommend lesser prison sentences providing extenuating circumstances are present. In cases of first degree murder, if the death penalty was out of the question, then a life sentence should be just that. One real observation I made since this happened to me is how the police are becoming increasingly disillusioned with the whole process. I will never criticise the police after seeing the amount of work they put into Alan's case. The detective in charge of the case actually left his position in Auckland to move north as he was so disheartened with the amount of violent crime and the incompetence of the system. And here's a question for our Members of Parliament. "Have any of you personally been affected by violent crime? Have you ever experienced a trial resulting from a violent crime affecting you, your family or friends?" Perhaps some of them might consider attending a trial to experience the distress of the family or watch a video of the defendant rather than read the sanitised version in the newspaper in the comfort of their lounge.

My marriage to Alan was my second and we had only been married 18 months. We were planning a family later in the year he was killed. Here I am back on my own, one child and myself to support. Mind you I did get an allowance from ACC but in reality it's a pathetic weekly payment for myself and daughter. We got a lump sum payment as well but it doesn't even cover the cost of a funeral. My husband died without a will or life insurance. I gave up my job to run Alan's business and now I have my own but I'm alone. I look at the future at 35 with some fear and disillusionment about possible future relationships and the path our society is taking. Not very comforting thoughts!

Perhaps relating my fears, concerns and emotions is therapeutic though far from easy. But then it's better than what was offered by the ACC. I recall an incident that made me very angry. At one stage, when I was at a particularly low ebb, I visited my doctor. When I broke down in his surgery he rang the ACC on my behalf. I needed and wanted counselling but financially it was out of my reach, and the Corporation's response? "Did she witness the murder?"

"No," replied my doctor.

"Well, I'm sorry but she would only be eligible for counselling if she witnessed it."

My final thoughts are for other victims. Every time I hear news of yet another murder I just feel so much sympathy for the victim and family for their loss, but most of all I feel sorry they will have to go through what I did. And in the end they too will probably face an outcome not befitting the seriousness of someone's life being taken.

19

Alicia O'Reilly

On the evening of 15 August, 1980, Nancye O'Reilly put her 6-year-old daughter Alicia to bed in her Auckland home. In the morning Alicia was discovered having been raped and murdered some time during the night. To date her murderer has not been found.

Many of the stories in this book talk of the despair families face when loved ones are murdered. But as Nancye O'Reilly has found, there can be an end to the nightmare. Fifteen years after the shocking murder of Alicia, Nancye's thoughts follow...

Life for the most part is comfortable. There is a renewed sense of purpose, a new set of beliefs, a feeling of being one but together with the universe. I have experienced its joys and its sadness, and I have journeyed down the road to hell and back.

Early on, life was about excitement and passion, about joy and love. Then life became death, pain, despair, loneliness and hatred.

Now it is about life and death, a new connection somehow. A peacefulness, a serenity and a knowledge of the spiritual that I had never known before.

No high highs and no low lows. Life does not surprise, and while it does not bring fear it has ceased to be carefree. What was thought to be mundane now brings pleasure.

Life is a gift and in an odd way I am thankful for the comparison between the positive and the negative. I no longer feel guilt about enjoying and loving life. I no longer feel the negativity that often overwhelmed me, and I now have a deep empathy and understanding of other people's pain. I see life as a jigsaw with the pieces slowly falling into place.

But there remains a missing part which still eludes me. The identity of the offender. The nameless, faceless person who robbed me of a carefree life. The actions that brought more pain, anger and fear than I had ever experienced before. He robbed me of my expectations, my celebrations and my role as a mother. He still intrudes from time to time.

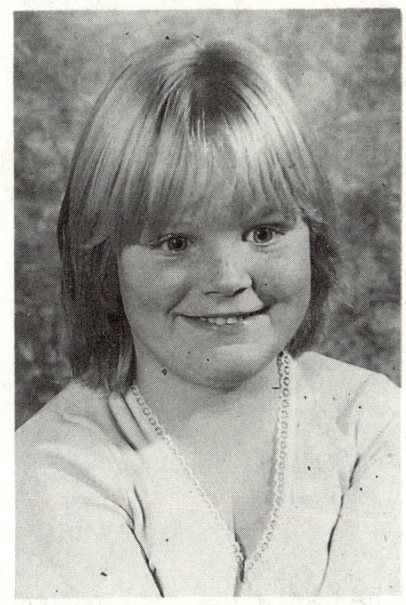

Alicia May O'Reilly, raped and murdered at just six years of age.

There is a promise that one day the pain will cease. Yet, while the pain does ease, it still brings a sadness. Memories awaken at a certain song or a particular flower, and depart leaving a longing for another time and another place. But now there are other tiny hands, not replacements, but treasured souls. Their faces alight with the joy and excitement of life. And their love erases the sadness.

Is there an end to the nightmare? Is there a life after a death? Yes! I now know there is.

The fact that Nancye can again find happiness is a tribute to her and those who have been able to support her. A little over seven years after Alicia was murdered, her eldest daughter Juliet, then aged 15, was killed by a drunk driver. Further tragedy struck in 1990 when baby Kimberley died six hours after being born. Nancye now lives in Auckland with a partner and two young sons.

20

The ACC

Throughout this book reference has been made to the need for homicide victims' families to be compensated. As in the case of Debbie Woodward, who lost most of her family in one terrible rampage by her brother-in-law Raymond Ratima, compensation does not mean a dollar value on someone's life. Compensation to her and others is simply a mechanism to provide for things such as counselling. There is little doubt that suffering the trauma of a loved one killed by a murderer requires specialist care to help overcome the effects and that specialist service does not come cheaply.

At last there is a facility to provide for counselling but it does not come from ACC. The moves underway to address the issue still have a way to go, but at last the needs are finally being acknowledged.

To understand the role of the ACC in cases of homicide we need to look at the history of compensation in criminal cases. By doing this we can understand the needs of people like Debbie Woodward and many others mentioned in this book. It also helps us understand the effects of inequities in cases such as the murder of Carol Pye. How could it be that our "system" can provide $500 for each of her children when they turn 20, yet pay out over $18,000 to her murderer for injuries received in a bungled attempt to escape from prison. The following is a precis of a paper entitled *Compensation for Victims of Crime: Do We Return to Criminal Injury Legislation?* The paper was written by Ike Williams, for his seminar in the LLB (Hons) course in Victimology taught by John Miller, Senior Lecturer in Law at Victoria University.

Victims of crime have been treated primarily like any other victim in New Zealand with compensation principally coming from Accident Compensation legislation. However there is a growing trend that crime victims have special needs and should be treated separately. This paper provides an historical background, a discussion of why victims should be compensated, a review of the present situation and finally a look at ways it could be improved.

Background
In the beginning wronged citizens relied on civil rather than criminal law for protection. The individual was considered to suffer the wrong and not the State, but the growth of royal and ecclesiastical authority in the Middle Ages contributed to the division between civil and criminal law.

By the 12th Century the victim's rights to reparation were largely replaced by fines paid to the state. As time went by more offences were considered crimes against society rather than the individual with victims largely becoming forgotten. Over the following centuries the victim was left to their own devices to get restitution, primarily by a civil claim for damages.

It was not until World War II that governments of the so called western world developed a moral conscience and started to recognise the rights and needs of the socially disadvantaged. The United Nations Declaration of Human Rights in 1948, which was principally aimed at preventing the repetition of Nazi atrocities during the war, was subsequently adopted as a charter for protection against discrimination and oppression of all kinds. Conventions were signed by many countries of the world which recognised the needs of the socially disadvantaged and as such the needs of crime victims slowly became recognised. At the same time society became richer and welfare arrangements steadily extended to victims of various disabilities and disadvantages. Crime victims were not far behind.

New Zealand led the way in 1963 with the introduction of the first criminal injuries compensation scheme. This was followed by similar legislation in Britain and in the following decade America, Canada, Australia and some members of the European community followed.

What's the justification for State compensation?
There is a generally accepted principle that there is a moral obligation by states to look after crime victims. This is backed up by the United Nations Declaration of Basic Principles of Justice for Victims of Crime and Abusive Power 1985 which states:

When compensation is not fully available from the offender or other sources, states should endeavour to provide financial compensation to victims who have sustained significant bodily injury or impairment of physical or mental health as a result of serious crime. Also victims should receive the necessary material, medical, psychological and social assistance through government, voluntary, community based and indigenous means.

New Zealand was a co-sponsor to this declaration. The Victim of Offences Act 1987 draws directly from it as can be seen in section 4 of the Act which states: The victims and, where needed, their families, should have access to welfare, health, counselling, medical and legal assistance responsive to their needs.

However, even though there was a moral consensus that compensation for crime victims was necessary, the theoretical justification remained obscure. There are three proposed theories that address these issues.

Firstly there is a theory that suggests the use of reparation is necessary in order for individuals to retain respect for the criminal justice system and not take the law into their own hands. Also it encourages victims to report offences and to cooperate with the police and courts if they know that a successful prosecution will enhance their claim for compensation.

Secondly there is a theory where it is argued that the state has a duty to protect its citizens from crime and that if it fails to do so it incurs the obligation to indemnify those who are victimized. The idea is that if society fails in this respect, then the social contract has been breached and the citizens have suffered. This idea has been criticised on the basis that the victim would then have a legal enforceable right to whatever level of compensation a court or official agency might determine and this would result in public expenditure outside political control. The counter-argument to this is that like health and education, the right to compensation is only an equitable share of what the government can reasonably afford.

There is also the justification put forward on the basis of equity. It has been suggested that it is unfair that victims should receive nothing from the state when substantial public expenditure is devoted to the apprehension, conviction and punishment of criminals. It is also unfair that help and relief is not given to victims of crime on a scale comparable with that given to sufferers from other forms of disadvantage or disability. The justification that human life and dignity are paramount social priorities is important. Compensation contributes to the continuance of the quality of life and the restoration of dignity. Since only the state has the resources to provide such compensation, the consequences of crime on the life and dignity of the victim impose a duty on the government to respond in this way.

The final theory is a combination of the two approaches resulting in the focus being upon the common good. Harm to the victim is seen as harm to society in general and society as a whole should bear it. Compensation is a means where the loss can be distributed across society as a whole. The promotion of such a concept is widely recognised as a proper objective to government and a way of promoting a greater happiness and wellbeing to citizens. The question is how best to achieve it and how far coverage should go.

What's available in New Zealand today?
Compensation for victims of crime may be from a number of sources depending on who the victim is and the type of injury suffered.

The Criminal Justice Act 1985
A victim is entitled to receive reparation under this Act. Under one section the court can sentence the offender to make reparation where they are satisfied that someone suffered emotional harm or loss or damage to property.

Section 22 is worded "to any other person" and this enables secondary victims who suffer emotional harm from witnessing a crime to be entitled to reparation from the offender, while section 28 is directed at the primary victim. Acknowledgement of the harm done and material reparation should come from the offender but there are a number of problems on this being the sole form of compensation to the victim. Firstly the lack of offender means. Nearly three-quarters of the cases that involve victim losses are committed by offenders who are unemployed and therefore unable to pay reparation. Judges feel this has hindered the use of the reparation sentence while at the same time it raised victims' expectations. Secondly enforcement is a problem with only about 53% of all sentences of reparation being paid in full. For the victim the promise of reparation which they never get can result in revictimisation. A similar problem arises with fines. This could be overcome by the creation of a State fund that bridges the gap and could be paid into by all offenders. Finally there is the problem for those victims of crime where the offender is never found and this is a reason to suggest something more is required.

The Accident Rehabilitation and Compensation Insurance Act 1992 (ARCIA)
The ARCIA basically provides for victims of crime for personal injury suffered in New Zealand, cover for personal injury caused by accident and any mental injury caused by physical injury.

The exception is for a victim of certain sexual crimes who may claim for mental consequences regardless of whether there are physical injuries or not. A victim can receive under the Act, earnings related compensation, medical and dental treatment resulting from the injury, an independence allowance, death benefits or rehabilitation.

General inadequacies of ARCIA
Earnings related compensation is inadequate as any loss of earnings is only compensated up to 80 percent. Although this is the same for all victims under ARCIA, the deliberate nature of the act makes it even more unjust to victims of crime. There is an independence allowance if the personal injury results in a degree of disability of 10 percent or more. But this is only to a maximum of $40 per week where a person is 100 percent disabled. If the disability is considered less than 10 percent the

victim receives nothing. It does not compensate the victim for the pain and suffering that results and in some cases this is considerable. This payment of an allowance can also serve as a constant reminder of the traumatic event if the victim is not capable of putting it behind them.

The allowance is based on the physical injury and any mental injury arising from it. This highlights the absurdity where a person's life may be ruined by the psychological consequences of a crime yet they receive no allowance. The Act places most of the responsibility on the person themselves to effect their own rehabilitation. There is no compensation for property damage that a victim may sustain as a result of the criminal act, nor is there coverage for expenses as a result of being involved in the court process. It is therefore debatable whether this is true compensation.

There are a number of victims the Act does not cover. Victims of crime that do not suffer physical injury, but suffer mental injury, nervous shock or stress that is not the result of a sexual offence receive no cover under the Act. These may be victims of assault and burglary and various other offences. Secondary victims of crime which generally include the victim's immediate family, but not necessarily confined solely to this, have no cover under the Act for nervous shock or stress they may suffer. This is contrary to the cover that section 4 of the Victim of Offences Act requires.

Criminal Justice Assistance Reimbursement
This is not a legislative right but a discretionary award determined by the Secretary of Justice. It provides cover for those who have been victimised and suffered loss of property or earnings because of their testimony to help as a witness for the prosecution or the defence in a criminal case that is punishable by imprisonment. It also covers assistance in the administration of justice such as giving information to the police without being called to court. If someone is in a close relationship with a witness and as a result of assisting they are victimised and suffer loss of property or earnings they will be compensated for their material loss. This has only been recently introduced and as yet has had little use.

145

Counselling for Families of Murder Victims

The National Council of Victim Support Groups has the discretionary power under a scheme where victim support groups throughout the country can advise families of their entitlement. The criteria for entitlement is difficult to attain. It is limited to family members or relationships of a family nature, and applicants have one year to lodge a claim from the time of discovery of the murder. This entitles a victim to 15 hours of counselling and upon approval a further 15 if required.

The two major pitfalls appear to be that the one year time-frame on lodging an application may eliminate counselling for many victims. Because of their involvement in the judicial process many victims may only begin to realise their grief and anger when there is no longer anything to focus on such as an enquiry or court case. This will not be a problem if the case is dealt with very quickly but murder cases often take more than a year to investigate and prosecute. One way is to encourage people to claim within the year and use it whenever they like. The second possible pitfall is where a person witnesses the murder but has no family ties and consequently is not eligible for counselling even though the trauma involved may be just as great. Close friends may not be classified as a relationship of a family nature.

Civil claims in relation to ARCIA

ARCIA restricts those people who can bring a civil action for damages. If the personal injury is covered by the Act one cannot sue for damages except for exemplary damages. All victims of crime who are covered are barred from bringing actions related to what ARCIA compensates them for.

Is the present cover adequate?

The answer is obviously no. The inconsistencies and inadequacies of the various forms of cover available to victims are numerous. Not only is it administratively a nightmare due to the various avenues available to a victim but there are a lot of pitfalls to be negotiated. The result means nothing for those who are not covered and inadequate cover for those who are.

What is the solution?

There are two alternatives. Either improve the present system or rectify the ARCIA anomalies to provide adequate cover for victims of crime. Failing that introduce a specific criminal injuries compensation legislation.

The first option would require specific reference to criminal injuries so as all situations are covered. The type of harm that is covered should include all types of emotional harm with or without associated physical harm. Compensation for pain and suffering should be included. The return of lump sum payments, even if only for victims of crime, or at the very least an assessment of the independence allowance that included solely mental injury. There also needs to be an extension of cover so that all secondary victims will receive compensation and a liberalisation of counselling so victims of crime can get what they require quickly. Specific provisions for property loss could be introduced where insurance does not cover it.

By extending ARCIA to cover all crime victims' needs would mean all compensation is available from one highly visible system that everyone is aware of. The procedures are already in place to enable efficient administration and any alterations could be limited to crime victims alone.

The alternative is to actually set up a separate compensation scheme that deals solely with victims of crime. This can be justified on the basis that victims of crime suffer a distinctive harm. The nature of how the harm is inflicted creates a lot more emotional and mental problems, very often there is a sense of being let down by society in general. Many victims of crime suffer crises due to the invasion of their own domain and there are often real fears of a recurrence. For many the ordeal continues through the administration of justice where special support and compensation is needed such as travelling expenses and possibly legal costs. Not just general counselling.

The wide range of victims such as witnesses who suffer loss through the justice process or families that become involved in it, are unique situations that do not fall within the objectives of ARCIA.

It would be possible to combine the two approaches as the Victims Task Force suggested. Set up a criminal injuries compensation board that determines the needs of the victims and the relevant compensation. It should be separately funded but still administered by the ARCIA.

A separate scheme for crime victims or section of them in ARCIA does raise a problem. Crime victims would undoubtedly be entitled to greater compensation because of the distinctive harm they would suffer. The danger is that if the type of crime is not specifically defined it may be possible to classify injuries as criminal when in reality they are accidental. For instance if someone was injured through a motor vehicle accident and the car did not have a warrant then it could be a criminal offence. If it was deemed to be a criminal injury it would entitle the victim to more compensation when it was really just an accident. To stop the purpose of separate cover for crime victims being defeated considerable thought would be needed in deciding the criteria to qualify for criminal injury compensation.

Conclusion
It is obvious that compensation for victims of crime in New Zealand is inadequate. For those that are covered, it is insufficient. Those that are left to retrieve their own compensation their chances are often defeated by a poor or unapprehended offender. Finally there is a significant group who have no way to get compensation at all. Regardless of one's viewpoint there is ample justification that victims of crime should be compensated to the extent suggested even if it is simply to meet our international obligations or the requirements of the Victim of Offences Act. Whether it is separate legislation or a modified ARCIA, victims of crime would receive the recognition and compensation that will assist them to resume a normal life.
Ike Williams, June 1995

One of the leading proponents of victims' rights and their battles to achieve adequate and realistic compensation is John Miller, a Barrister and Senior Lecturer in Law at Wellington's Victoria University. For some years John has taken on cases such as the Pam Cochrane case. He has not charged for his services and through his persistence and expertise the judge found in Pam's favour. This opened the door for the kind of considerations people had been hoping for. The following statement comes from John Miller himself.

In November 1991 I had just finished being interviewed on radio on some ACC matter when I received a phone call from

Odette Leather in Auckland. She had heard the interview and said she was a member of the Citizens Against Violence organisation – a group whose members, apart from Odette, were the immediate family members of homicide victims. Odette explained she had been assisting members of the group to claim counselling costs and compensation from the ACC for the mental trauma they had suffered. Initially the claims were successful but the ACC had changed their policy and was no longer recognising them.

The reason for the change had been a 1991 decision in the High Court by Justice Holland in a case named ACC v F which was totally unrelated to homicide victims. The F case dealt with a husband's claim for mental trauma which he suffered from no longer being able to have sex with his wife as she had suffered a personal injury by accident. Justice Holland had rejected the husband's claim on various grounds, one of them being that the husband was trying to claim for an accident suffered by another (his wife). The ACC had started using this case to say that the same result applied in homicide cases as well. That the mental trauma suffered by survivors from the death of the family member was another case of someone relying on a accident to another – the deceased. It should be explained at this point that the law has always regarded intentional killings as coming within the definition of an accident. That definition is an untoward event which is not expected or designed.

As a result of this change in ACC policy Odette was having to fight the various claims on appeal through to the Accident Compensation Appeal Authority. However if she lost at the Appeal Authority level the next step would be an appeal to the High Court where she would need a barrister to take the case. Hence her phone call to me.

Because I considered the ACC policy to be totally wrong and harsh I readily agreed to take the case on a free basis. This is not uncommon, many members of the legal profession (outside larger firms) take cases on a free basis. However I do more free work than other lawyers as, unlike them, I do not have the expense of running a practice. I also consider that taking court cases makes me a more effective researcher and teacher and it gives me an opportunity to try and change the law for the better. Furthermore I consider that university staff should set an example to our law students by doing this type of work, hence my offer of free assistance.

One month later, in December 1991 Odette contacted me with the recently issued Accident Compensation Appeal Authority decision rejecting the claim of Pam Cochrane. Pam's son had been horribly beaten and tortured by members of a gang who had then dumped him outside Waikato Hospital. Pam was called to the hospital and was at her son's side for the 20 hours he suffered until he died. Because of his injuries and pain she was not allowed to even hold him in those final hours. The ACC and the Appeal Authority had rejected her claim on the basis that ACC only covered claims for personal injury by accident and that as only Pam's son had suffered the accident she could not claim on the accident suffered by another.

I considered this to be totally wrong. Given that an accident had been defined in previous cases as an untoward event which is not expected or designed Pam had clearly suffered this. Indeed to call what happened to Pam as an untoward event is far too mild – it is the event every parent dreads.

To appeal to the High Court one has to get permission from the Appeal Authority and I applied for this on 7 January 1992. However it was not until May 1992 that I obtained leave to appeal and filed the Notice in the High Court. It then took another two months until July 1992 to get the ACC to complete the appropriate forms stating that the case was ready for hearing. We then had a long wait on a court date in the High Court for a full day hearing and unfortunately that did not arrive for over a year – 23 August 1993. Fortunately after listening to a full day of argument by myself for Pam and two lawyers from a large legal firm for the ACC, Justice Greig issued a judgement straight away in Pam's favour.

He decided that provided there was medical evidence of mental trauma then secondary victims such as Pam would be covered by ACC as they had suffered their own personal injury by accident. However the ACC still refused to accept this decision and applied for leave from the High Court to appeal to the Court of Appeal. This involved another argument in the High Court on 14 December 1993 where Justice Greig refused the ACC leave to appeal to the Court of Appeal. The only option left to the ACC was to apply to the Court of Appeal directly for special leave to appeal but fortunately good sense at last prevailed and on 24 December 1993 they advised me that they would not be proceeding further.

The Pam Cochrane decision thus allowed many other claims to be recognised. At the time of the decision there was a large number of claims with the ACC still waiting for an initial decision. Some 28 claims were also at the review stage and over 20 appeals were before the Accident Compensation Appeal Authority. These were all paid out.

Unfortunately the decision only applied to all the claims that had been made before 1 July 1992 as the Accident Rehabilitation and Compensation Insurance Act 1992 came into force on that date. This clearly excluded claims for such mental trauma from secondary victims of crimes. To partially meet this gap left by the 1992 Act the government has recently provided limited funds for counselling for the families of murder victims.

As they are no longer covered by ACC such victims now also have rights to sue the criminals for damages for their mental trauma but in most cases that will not be worthwhile as most criminals have no assets or income. Even if covered by ACC crime victims have always had the right to sue for what is known as exemplary damages to punish the criminal but this has rarely been done as it is not financially viable.

It is clear that most crime victims and all the families of crime victims are now neglected by ACC even though they are recognised by the Victims of Offences Act 1987 and are recognised by Criminal Injuries Compensation schemes worldwide. New Zealand was the first country to have a Criminal Injuries Compensation scheme in 1963 but we abandoned it when the ACC scheme came in 1974 believing it was no longer necessary. Instead we now have the mean spirited 1992 Act in force and we either have to improve ACC again or set up a new criminal injuries compensation scheme.

Sadly Odette Leather who brought me into this work died on 14 October 1994. I took over the few remaining files she was still working on to try and secure compensation and counselling for homicide victims' families. Shortly after her death I was working on the files when I suddenly felt the need to contact a Gisborne family whose daughter had been killed. Odette had always been particularly concerned about this family. They answered the phone and were amazed that I was ringing as they had been reaching for the phone at the same time to phone me. We both put it down to Odette still watching over us and willing us to carry on her work.

I am still prepared to provide free legal advice, research and action for crime victims. I can call on the assistance of students, particularly those who have taken my course in victimology at Victoria University. We hope to eventually set up a centre at the university for free legal advice, research and action for crime victims. In the meantime, anyone requiring legal assistance should contact me at the Faculty of Law, Victoria University, PO Box 600, Wellington, phone (04) 495-5217 or fax (04) 495-5236.

John Miller, September 1995

Compensation for the families of murder victims is still an issue for the future. Although some counselling is being provided by government and despite the future looking more certain there is still considerable work to be done. There is no doubt that families of murder victims do need help and that the obligation for that assistance rests with the State.

21

Where to from here?

For hundreds of years the criminal justice system geared itself towards the apprehension and punishment of offenders. The whole system revolved around the principle of the State prosecuting the offender who was, in most cases, defended by a lawyer. Those who could not afford a defence would still be represented through court appointed legal aid solicitors.

While there is no contention that people being prosecuted should have competent representation in court, the argument has been that the emphasis put on the right to a defence is often at odds with the rights of a victim. For instance there is no right for a family who have lost a loved one through murder to be represented in court. During the defence of the alleged murderer all sorts of allegations can be cast about the character of the deceased. Often we hear from the defence that the deceased somehow was the author of their own misfortune, that they were in part to blame for their demise, or that their character was such that perhaps the offender could be absolved of some of the blame. Allegations which are often unsubstantiated could easily be refuted but the prosecution, on behalf of the family, doesn't get the opportunity.

It is devastating for parents to lose their daughter in a sexually motivated murder. But imagine how galling it is to hear imputations that put their daughter's character in doubt. Those are the types of situations that led to a strong call for victim advocacy.

Since 1987 there has been a concerted move towards victims' rights. Once the Victims of Offences Act was passed and the Victims Task Force set up the "system" slowly changed. Victims are at last being heard and supported from the initial stage of a crime having been committed through to the court case and beyond. In cases of homicide special provisions were made which augur well for the future. However, like many good initiatives, there is a need to keep going forward. Over the past decade there have been tremendous moves towards a greater equality for victims but there is still room for improvement. Many of the concerns people hold have been mentioned in the individual stories in this book. But while there have been significant advances to correct the balance there is still a long way to go.

Parole

The parole of long term prisoners, especially those convicted of murder, has been a concern for many people. Those who have lost loved ones to a murder find it incomprehensible that a life sentence might mean 10 years.

Parole boards are made up of a cross-section of the community who decide on when an inmate should be released. Their decisions are based on the information given them by the Justice Department.

Victims can have an input into that decision making process, but at the invitation of the parole board chairperson. If the victims get the opportunity to make submissions they do so knowing that the offender will be given all information put before the board. In cases of murder those making submissions have seen what the offender is capable of doing and this in itself can be quite traumatic.

Groups such as Family and Friends of Murder Victims believe parole provisions need formalising. If the offender can get access to all information concerning their case so too should the victim. If they are to be part of the decision making process, shouldn't they know what therapy, courses or other corrective measures the offender has undertaken? Was it imposed or voluntary? Has he really made an effort to rehabilitate or will he pose the same threat once released? While these may not be questions of great relevance to many people, they are uppermost in the victim's mind.

Victim of Offences Act 1987

This Act was introduced in 1986 as a private member's bill by the then

Minister of Justice the Hon J McLay but was defeated.

Following community pressure, applied principally through the lobby group Citizens Against Violence, the Victims of Offences Act came into force in 1987. The modified act introduced by the Hon Geoffrey Palmer was based on the principles of the United Nations Declaration of the Rights of Victims of Crime and Abuse of Power. New Zealand had been a co-sponsor to that declaration.

For two reasons the Act was very important. Firstly it set up the Victims Task Force and secondly it wrote into law guidelines for how victims should be treated, though it failed to offer remedies. Although the first chairperson of the Task Force was Denise Blake of the Department of Justice, her secondment to Canada soon after the Task Force was established saw the reins handed to a former psychologist at the University of Canterbury. Ann Ballin had just finished a term on the Royal Commission on Social Policy when she was appointed to the chair of the Victims Task Force and carried on in that position until the group was finally disbanded in 1993. For her outstanding efforts to the community and mainly for her work on the Victims Task Force, Ann Ballin was made a Dame in 1993.

The Act itself provided real recognition of victims' rights, for example victim impact statements. These are statements that put before a sentencing judge any physical or emotional harm or loss of or damage to property suffered by the victim. This has been tremendously successful in the move to help victims. At last they were able to have their views considered and judges are now taking more cognisance of those effects when passing sentence or considering reparation.

There are now provisions where victims are given information about the progress of an investigation, what charges are laid, and if none are laid why not. The role the victim has in the process and details of any trials should be given to them in sufficient time to prepare. This does not always happen though there is no reason why that should be so. One criticism victims had was how they were often kept in the dark, which in turn took away their belief that a case was in fact theirs. As the wheels of justice turned, the assault or burglary they suffered ceased to be "their" assault or burglary. More often it belonged to the police, the prosecutor, the judge or whoever. Armed with information about their case, and taking into account their views, it empowered victims who felt they now had some control over what was taking place.

Victims views on bail in cases of sexual violence and serious assault can now be considered, and if a victim has real fears for their safety then they have a right to have those fears considered. Whether they are taken into account is a matter for the judge.

Two principles of the Act were particularly important. Firstly the members of the police, prosecution, judicial officers, counsel, officials and other persons dealing with victims should treat them with courtesy, compassion and respect for their personal dignity and privacy. For years victims were the forgotten part of the equation and often felt that they were the ones on trial. Waiting nervously to give evidence whilst sitting in a waiting room with friends and relatives of the accused should be a thing of the past.

The second important principle was for victims, and where needed their families, to have access to welfare, health, counselling, medical and legal assistance. As yet many of these support mechanisms are still out of reach as most cost money which is still lacking. In April 1995 the Government made a significant move making $500,000 available for the counselling of families of murder victims. This scheme, administered by victim support groups under contract to the Community Funding Agency, will go a long way to help those affected overcome the emotional pressures of coping with such horrific crimes as murder. Funding is provided from 1% of paid fines and, as the Courts are now putting pressure on people to pay, the available amount should increase. Family members and those in close relationships to the murder victim will now be able to get up to six initial counselling sessions or up to 15 after an assessment determines the need. This is one initiative that has a direct bearing on the family of murder victims and is much applauded.

We are a long way ahead of what support was available only a few years ago and no doubt the future will bring about further positive action.

The Victims Task Force

The Victims Task Force was never intended to be a permanent body yet was so successful at generating interest for victims' rights that many people felt something was needed to keep the momentum going. Over the term of the Task Force, New Zealand saw quite a revolutionary change. Prior to 1986 there was virtually nothing that specifically saw to the needs of victims apart from traditional support groups like women's refuge and rape crisis. Several overseas countries had grasped the victims concept and were working particularly well. The National Organisation for Victims' Assistance (NOVA) in the United States had very strong support groups with large budgets. Late in 1990 the director of NOVA visited New Zealand and helped with the direction of victim support groups here.

NOVA were specialists, not only in direct victim support, but also crisis intervention. That concept was well illustrated when, exactly seven days after the NOVA director visited Dunedin, the nearby settlement of Aramoana was torn apart by a lone gunman during a shooting rampage. The ripple effect of that tragedy was felt strongly in the township of Port Chalmers and even extended right throughout Dunedin and into Otago and across the rest of the country.

The Task Force, through a persistent and knowledgeable chairperson, was responsible for many changes to law and attitude. For example the introduction of the Children, Young Persons and Their Families Act saw provision for victims to be represented at family group conferences. The responsibility to see this is in fact done would be one of the prime responsibilities of a commissioner for victims.

One of the main conditions for offenders being eligible for the police diversion scheme is that the victim agrees. Diversions are for first offenders appearing on relatively minor charges. If they acknowledge their guilt and show genuine remorse then the police can withdraw the information from court. The offender will either agree to some voluntary community work or pay a sum of money to an approved charity. Doing this they atone for their indiscretions while at the same time avoid a criminal conviction. However this can only happen if the victim agrees.

Probably the greatest legacy of the Victims Task Force was their input into encouraging the development of victim support groups. Prior to the setting up of the Task Force, victim support groups, or the concept, were little more than a flicker. Within seven years more than 70 groups with a strong national body were set up. That successful move and the incredible speed with which victim support groups expanded was because of the dedicated people whose hard work carried the momentum along. All groups were, and still are, supported in many ways by the police who got behind the movement with policy, finance and above all a change in attitude from offender orientated to an empathy with victims.

Victim Support Groups

Each victim support group is autonomous and works on its own accord. However they are affiliated to the national body, have recognised structures and codes of practice and are funded by the Community Funding Agency. When one talks of victim support it is not only those groups affiliated to the New Zealand Council. There are others doing tremendous work in this field. For example the long-standing traditional groups like women's refuges and rape crisis centres carry out vitally important roles in specific areas of victim support. So too do groups such as Family and Friends of Murder Victims. That group, for whom this book was written, still carry out support and have a network for those families devastated by murder. Groups such as this go way beyond the physical support of victims. They play an important role in bringing issues to public attention and generating political change. Almost everyone and every group in New Zealand, working for the rights of victims, rely on meagre budgets and the widespread use of volunteers.

Late in 1995 a new group was formed, an initiative of the New Zealand Police Association. VICTIMNZ is based on a successful Canadian system and has on its board Dame Ann Ballin and Debbie Francis, one of the founders of Family and Friends of Murder Victims.

VICTIMNZ hope to unite the many groups working on victims' issues. Unity of purpose is seen as important, especially in the early stages of what is still a relatively new concept. The VICTIMNZ initiative also aims to promote change to legislation and policy especially in respect to bail laws and sentencing. Overall the aim is to see that the same rights given to offenders are extended to victims. The VICTIMNZ trust does not intend running any one group but instead will be a lobby group to encourage change. Central to its proposals is a common database which can be used to back up law changes, a facility any groups working in the victims' field can access. In the near future VICTIMNZ hopes to employ draftspeople to help with changes to laws to ensure victims' needs are met.

Although New Zealand still has some way to go, we are far from lagging behind the rest of the world. At the 8th International Symposium on Victimology held in Adelaide in August 1994 it was quite apparent that any ground we had lost by our late start has been quickly made up. Few countries head us when it comes to victims' rights and many countries envy where we have got to.

Commissioner for Victims

When the Task Force went out of existence there was a strong recommendation to replace it with a Commissioner for Victims. To date this has not happened. Although the members of the Task Force and many people working in victim support are sure a commissioner is a logical step the Government has yet to be convinced. It believes that funding is better directed at providing frontline services to victims through government agencies and organisations. This seems a logical move but when one considers the funding available, despite the tremendous push for victims' rights, there is still inequality. The Victims Task Force was originally funded with 1% of paid fines. Logically one could expect that funding for victims should come from the offenders by way of fines. Even if only 5% of fines was directed to victims' issues there should be sufficient to establish an office for a commissioner for victims. To use lack of funding as a criteria for holding back on such a strong recommendation is rather suspect. Lack of a centralised, independent policy body to coordinate victims' issues is keenly felt. Perhaps the new Court's Division of Justice, who administers victims' issues, can do the job adequately. Then again the question of victims' issues might be a bigger task than they can handle. And in any event the commissioner concept must be independent of both Justice and groups working in the victims' field.

Despite the reluctance of Government to appoint a commissioner for victims, support groups around the country are asking for this office to be established and a private member's bill is soon to be introduced to Parliament in this regard. There is no doubt that in just eight years the growth of victim support in New Zealand has been dramatic, but there is a long way to go and a government appointed office, such as that proposed, would ensure the movement stays on track.

Homicide Trained Victim Support

Victim support in New Zealand provides assistance for a wide range of victims. Many people need help, and not just for a supposed serious crime. What might be considered a 'minor' burglary of a house where an elderly woman lives alone might have just as much or more victim impact than a huge commercial enterprise losing thousands of dollars in a professional burglary. Victim support should be, and is, aimed at the impact on the individual. Support groups throughout the country have details of people suffering traumatic experiences from what were, in the past, regarded as minor crimes.

Perhaps the most devastating of all crimes is a case of murder. Victim support groups quickly realised that this class of victim needed more specialised help, not only through the initial upheaval and often media intensive enquiry but throughout the court process and beyond. It's not uncommon for a year to pass from the time a murder is discovered until the offender is finally sentenced.

Because of the volunteer nature of victim support it was unlikely the same volunteer could attend to someone's ongoing needs – it was common to have different support people coming into the victim's life.

With specially trained volunteers in homicide work available, the impact on victims can be reduced as long as the families' special needs are recognised and acknowledged. The key to success is an ability to listen. This move of having specially trained homicide volunteers has been well received by victims, police and the courts and is now an integral part of homicide practice.

Victims Court Assistants

One of the most traumatic experiences a victim faces is having to appear in court and face their offender. In some cases, particularly those of sexual and violent crimes, the victim feels as if they are going through the ordeal again. They have minimal support and because of our ageing courtrooms and the way they were built it is common for a victim to come face to face with either the offenders directly or their family and friends. It is not uncommon to see a victim sitting on one side of a waiting room being eyeballed by members of a gang whose 'mate' is being prosecuted. As if the court process wasn't enough, giving evidence and being vigorously cross-examined can be a shattering experience.

A scheme introduced in 1994 saw an initiative of the Justice Department to enable victims to get through the judicial process with real support. Six pilot projects were set up throughout the country and quickly showed how effective they could be. Long-neglected needs of victims were at last being met. Now victims could feel they were part of the criminal justice system and that it really was 'their' case being heard, not the police's, not the Crown's.

Finally here was a system that was geared to keeping victims informed every step of the way with professional people at hand who knew the court system and all of the players within it. Where the role of Victims Court Assistants was generally one of providing information and support, the role quickly established other needs such as advocacy for victims. Clients of a Victims Court Assistant can now have a more direct input into opposition to bail, sentencing decisions, diversion and parole conditions and getting notified of when an offender might be released.

Preparation of victim impact statements, which judges take account of in coming to their sentencing decisions, is another important task of the Victims Court Assistant. Issues that victims have long anguished over are now being addressed.

Security, not only physical, but a belief victims feel secure is another important role and courtrooms of the future will have waiting rooms for witnesses and separate rooms for victims. So successful has the pilot scheme been that Victims Court Assistants will be set up around the country in 1996. This is one initiative that has direct and lasting benefits for those who have suffered.

If there is one area that needs strengthening it is more direct advocacy. It is fine to put one's views across as regards the effects of crime on an individual, but in cases such as murder there is still no facility to reject untrue allegations made by defence counsel regarding the movements, character or other contentious statements about the deceased. Greater advocacy of victims is an issue for the future but sooner rather than later.

The ultimate would be a true legal officer who could hold a watching brief and intervene on matters of information and procedure. At present no one questions pre-sentence reports which often contain false information upon which a judge partly bases his sentence. Under the Victims Court Assistant pilot scheme it was interesting to note in some cases where a judge, seemingly disbelieving a defence contention, asked for the other side of the story. Signs for true advocacy are there and this is one issue worth fighting for.

Degrees of Murder

Criminologists and those who study the topic have for years debated the question of punishment. Regardless of what degree of punishment is imposed anywhere in the world, the crime rate continues to advance. Perhaps the latest 'theory' to test crime on society is that of restorative justice. Essentially it means looking for an alternative to expensive imprisoning to find a cheaper, more effective way of firstly punishing transgressors while at the same time hoping to rehabilitate them.

Restorative justice seeks to bring about a reconciliation of victims and offenders with the community. To a degree this is what is done in family group conferences with young people and on many occasions it works. However the concept of restorative justice cannot occur unless offenders are made accountable for their actions and the victims are fully compensated. This concept has considerable merit. If someone burgles a house and steals a video, and is subsequently caught and held accountable for their actions the system works. If the victim gets a replacement video the system works.

But how does one apply restorative justice in cases of murder? Quite simply it cannot be done, and to this end suitable sentences either as punishment or as a deterrent must follow. Countries like America have for a long time had a system recognising degrees of murder. In New Zealand we have had, since capital punishment was abolished, a mandatory life imprisonment sentence for all murderers. There is little doubt that no one deserves to be murdered and it is difficult to say one case is more serious than another without minimising individual cases. But equally there are cases which are so heinous that little short of a life term, meaning life, is deserved. In reality there are degrees of murder but they are not recognised in law. Every conviction for murder endures the same punishment of life which in effect means the offender can be eligible for parole after 10 years.

The Crimes Act 1961 provided for life sentences for murder. The Government's position is that the present law should strike an appropriate balance. The Criminal Justice Act of 1985 now allows the sentencing judge to order, in exceptional cases, that a life sentence offender serve a minimum period of more than 10 years before becoming eligible for parole. There is no statutory limit on the duration of minimum period which the court can impose. This provision will go a long way towards ensuring offenders of more serious and exceptional cases of murder are made accountable but only if it is used to effect. It has been used on numerous occasions in the first year of it coming into existence but arguments have already surfaced as to what constitutes 'exceptional crimes'.

From the various policies of the political parties it is quite clear that no one has the answer and this has been the case for hundreds of years. Restorative versus punitive justice might be a noble aim but in cases of violent offending including aggravated robbery, rape and murder it is difficult to reconcile the two views. Perhaps the simple answer is to remove the words 'so exceptional' from the act and allow judges to give non parole periods for all murders. Then a sentence will be based on the nature of each case. In any event aren't all murders exceptional?

The Petition in Retrospect

When the petition was presented to Parliament, hopes were high that action would be taken in respect to sentencing murderers and the granting of bail or otherwise for serious sexual offenders. Although the petition was effectively 'shelved' many things have happened that can, in some way, be attributed to the petition which undoubtedly raised awareness of the issues. The moves in 1995 to provide minimum periods before parole can be considered for 'exceptional' murders, and the provision for counselling of family members are two examples.

The petition was considered by the Justice and Law Reform Select Committee who subsequently recommended the Government consider it. The Government, which shared the petitioners' concerns about serious crime in the community, gave careful consideration to the proposals. However the Government felt that imposing life sentences, which meant life, posed difficulties, believing some offenders would be punished out of proportion to the seriousness of their offending, hence the arguments against arbitrary sentencing or degrees of murder.

On the question of bail the premise that people are presumed innocent until proven guilty was the over-riding factor and the Government believes the discretion of courts to grant bail should remain. In a 1990 study only 2.2 percent of violent offenders reoffended in a violent way while on bail. Bail laws were however tightened in 1991 restricting bail for persons charged with or convicted of murder or specified violent or sexual offences. Bail is now precluded in those circumstances unless the offender can satisfy the judge that they will not commit offences of violence that endanger others. Regrettably Paul David Bailey could have fitted this category yet was able to murder Kylie Smith. Little wonder that the petitioners called for further tightening of bail provisions for sexual offenders. In assessing whether or not to grant bail the law provides that the need to protect the public shall be paramount.

Conclusion

This book has been about the experiences of families who have suffered the trauma of a murder and are but a handful of cases that appear in any one year. New Zealand has an unenviable record of homicide and only through the efforts of people like the three Owaka women, whose persistence in pushing for rights of the victims, will we see the balance swing towards equity.

For too long the emphasis has been in the wrong direction. For too long the offenders had all the rights of justice, bill of rights, access to legal aid or whatever. When the Victims Task Force wrote its report to the Minister of Justice they entitled their report 'Towards Equality in Criminal Justice.' Maybe victims are finally getting equality. But it's not yet there. Groups like Family and Friends of Murder Victims are determined to fight on to ensure that the equality and changes they have advocated do come about. Encouraging signs are at last starting to emerge but they cannot sit back and say there is nothing left to achieve.

Others are becoming interested in the pursuit of victims' issues. The manifestos of most political parties make specific mention of victims. Accident and Emergency departments in hospitals are training staff to support victims of crime by encouraging them to seek help. The judiciary are having an input into policy and the New Zealand Law Society has set up a victims' committee.

Perhaps the final thought goes back to the full page advertisement in the Sunday Times of 31 January, 1993 encouraging people to watch TV3's 20/20 programme about the murder of Kylie Smith and the two sentences in the advertisement: IF KYLIE CRIED FOR HELP AS SHE WAS BEING RAPED, NOBODY HEARD. IS ANYONE LISTENING NOW? Perhaps they are!

22

Conclusion

This book was written at the suggestion of the group Family and Friends of Murder Victims. It is therefore important that the final words come from them. They realise their work is far from over and summarise the issues they believe are not yet resolved.

In an effort to be 'fair' and 'just' a system has gradually evolved that is more concerned with the rights of the accused, and, if found guilty, the needs of the prisoner rather than those of the victims.

The Victims of Offences Act was introduced after pressure by the lobby group Citizens Against Violence led by the indomitable Odette Leather. This was the first step towards recognising that victims have rights.

Recently the government has recognised that homicide victims' families have some specific needs and introduced new initiatives to deal with this. In order to help these families we must first ascertain what their needs are and then consult with them as to how they can be adequately addressed. It is not good enough for academics to dictate their needs.

Some areas of the justice system still of concern to our group are:

Life sentence

The justice system is full of terms that do not mean what they imply and are often misleading to the public. An example is the time one actually serves in prison. LIFE means simply that the parole board has the power to ensure that the offender will stay in jail for 'LIFE'. However, in reality this is not the case. After serving 10 years the offender is able to apply for parole and if unsuccessful may apply every year following. In most cases they are released after serving 12 years. Another important fact to remember is that because an offender has only one 'LIFE' any other offences committed, i.e. if he raped then murdered, he will be sentenced to a concurrent term for the second offence. Concurrent simply means that both offences will be served together rather than one sentence being added to the other.

Degrees of murder

Family and Friends of Murder Victims Inc believe that some offenders, because of violent anti-social acts, have forfeited the right to live in society. It is for this reason our group would like to see degrees of murder introduced into our justice system. The penalty for a first degree murder being for the natural life of the person sentenced.

Non parole periods

In cases of murder/manslaughter, if the crime is carried out in a way that a judge perceives it to be 'so exceptional' he has the power to impose a non-parole period that must be served. The judge can sentence to 10, 20 or even 50 years or more before the offender will be eligible for parole. Recently an offender convicted of murdering his entire family (and currently appealing) was sentenced to a non-parole term of 15 years. Did this reflect the severity of the crime he committed or the number of people he murdered? Our group does not think so!

Judges

Family and Friends of Murder Victims Inc believes judges should be elected to office and not by government appointments. This should provide some measure of accountability.

Commissioner for victims

This was a Victims Task Force recommendation and something Odette Leather and Citizens Against Violence lobbied for. When Citizens Against Violence joined with Family and Friends of Murder Victims Inc we took up the cause for a Commissioner for Victims with

Victim Support Groups more recently adding their voice to the call. There is nowhere for victims to take complaints they may have about any agency dealing with them and there is an urgent need for an independent commissioner to whom they can take complaints.

Delay in trials

During 1995 the delay in trials resulted in some prosecutions being dropped because it would be unfair to the accused to proceed. The Crown wrote to the victims apologising, but in cases of sexual violation and violence an apology does not help. When somebody is accused of murder it is common for the trial to take a year or more to get to court and this adds to the trauma for families.

Parole board

At present families of homicide victims are able to put in submissions when an offender applies for parole. This is a courtesy extended to them by the parole board and something our group would like to see formalised by law. Under the Official Information Act the offenders have the right to access any information concerning their appearance including any submissions made by the families. This same right should apply to the victims and their families and they should have any information about the offender made available to them.

Representation in court

Representation in court is starting to be addressed. Victims can make submissions in writing to the court regarding bail and sentencing. They cannot however refute any statements in court they know to be untrue. Defence too often tries to gain the sympathy of the court by trying to blame the victim for what happened. Often the character of the deceased is called into question in an effort to absolve the offender. The prosecution does not work on behalf of the victim, but rather for the state and it is not part of their job to defend the victim's character. There is clearly a need for the families of homicide victims to have some sort of advocacy in the court room to challenge the defence's/ accused's statements.

Compensation

Often families of homicide victims are financially disadvantaged because of the violent criminal actions of another person. It may be that the principal wage earner for a family has been murdered. In the case of a child it may be that the wage earner, because of this horrendous act, is unable to perform at work. Most people incur costs

...nding the trial. In some Australian states lump sum ...tion is paid. New South Wales has recently brought in ...on for lump sum payments regardless of whether the offender ...ecuted or even caught. We would like New Zealand to recognise ...great wrong that has been done to these families by introducing ...mp sum payments.

Counselling

Family and Friends of Murder Victims Inc lobbied hard for counselling for homicide victims' families and a new initiative has been introduced by government. Although we have some reservations as to the guidelines for this scheme it is a tremendous step forward in recognising the needs of this group of victims.

We would like to pay special tribute to the late Odette Leather, who spent many years fighting for justice for homicide victims' families. Odette was loved and respected by all who met her and we feel privileged to have known her. Our admiration also goes to the families who have contributed to this book. We know the courage it has taken to speak out in the hope that changes will be made.